MY SECRET FISHING LIFE

BOOKS BY NICK LYONS

THE SEASONABLE ANGLER

JONES VERY: SELECTED POEMS (editor)

FISHERMAN'S BOUNTY (editor)

THE SONY VISION

LOCKED JAWS

FISHING WIDOWS

TWO FISH TALES

BRIGHT RIVERS

CONFESSIONS OF A FLY FISHING ADDICT

TROUT RIVER (text for photographs by Larry Madison)

SPRING CREEK

A FLYFISHER'S WORLD

MY SECRET FISH-BOOK LIFE

SPHINX MOUNTAIN AND BROWN TROUT

HEMINGWAY'S MANY-HEARTED FOX RIVER

IN PRAISE OF WILD TROUT (editor)

THE QUOTABLE FISHERMAN (compiler)

MY SECRET FISHING LIFE

MY SECRET
FISHING LIFE

Nick Lyons

Drawings by Mari Lyons

ATLANTIC MONTHLY PRESS • NEW YORK

Published simultaneously in Canada
Printed in the United States of America

FIRST EDITION

Library of Congress Cataloging-in-Publication Data

Lyons, Nick.
    My secret fishing life / Nick Lyons ; drawings by Mari Lyons.
        p.   cm.
    ISBN 0-87113-750-X
    1. Fishing—Anecdotes.   2. Lyons, Nick.   I. Title.
SH441.L945   1999
799.1—dc21
                                                            99-13921
                                                            CIP

Atlantic Monthly Press
841 Broadway
New York, NY 10003

99 00 01 02   10 9 8 7 6 5 4 3 2 1

For Mari—
again and again,
after forty years

CONTENTS

ACKNOWLEDGMENTS

My thanks to John Randolph and Philip Hanyok of *Fly Fisherman* for having given me the last page of their fine magazine; to Duncan Barnes for warmly encouraging me to write for *Field & Stream,* the magazine that lit my childhood; to John Merwin for publishing "Bad Sport" when it had been dropped at another magazine and rejected at several others as showing a "low view" of the sport; to Tom Taylor for his beautiful edition of *My Secret Fish-Book Life;* to Kevin Begos for his handsome edition of *Sphinx Mountain and Brown Trout.* And my gratitude to Eric Price and Morgan Entrekin, for their willingness to publish this book and to reprint four of my previous books on fishing. I value their confidence hugely.

Portions of this book originally appeared, sometimes in another form or with a different title, as follows:

Fly Fisherman Magazine: "A Fly Fisher's Spring," "Messing About in Boats a Little," "Going and Coming Back," "The 193 Minutes," "Journal Entries," "On the Top," "Truth in Outdoor Writing," "Me, Too," "Head Waters," "The Aging Fly Fisher," "Fishing, Yea, Yea," and portions of "My Fish-Book Life" and "Sphinx Mountain and Brown Trout."

The New York Times: "Diamond Jigging Near Wall Street," "Last Day," an early version of "Head Waters," and the portion of "My Secret Fish-Book Life" dealing with "rejection," which appeared in the *Times Book Review* section.

Field & Stream Magazine: "The Judge's Swim Pond," "Numbers Change," "Connections."

Fly Rod & Reel Magazine: "Bad Sport"

"Sphinx Mountain and Brown Trout" appeared as a book with that title published by Kevin Begos, and "My Fish-Book Life" appeared in an earlier version as a book called *My Secret Fish-Book Life,* published by W. Thomas Taylor.

PREFACE

I am fishing in riskier waters in this book than I have ever fished before. Fishing and painting, business and leisure, very short essays and book-length explorations, more of my personal life than I've let out of the vault before, and more that is made up, imagined—I have tried to include all this and a bit more this time. I have lived these various lives—all linked by my odd and enduring passion for fishing—in one skin; and I have tried hard to account for them all in this book, possibly my last on fishing.

Though fishing is my glue, and the fly fisher is the side of me I have always exposed most—partly because of the unalloyed pleasure I take from it, not only from the fishing but also from my writing about fishing—I have tried here to show how it connects to those other selves. This preoccupation with myself is a narrow turf, indeed, and compounding the narrowness is my compulsion to retread the same small plot over and over, constantly reworking old themes to have them make more sense to me, repeatedly finding new themes along old paths I've walked before, shifting and juggling, tinkering in words with a life I can't seem to get quite straight. I find myself not only looking at myself in the mirror, trying to catch that odd fellow in the glass unawares and truthfully, but also looking into the mirror of memory, of the past, which shimmers and changes like water in motion, and seems always to appear to me different from what it was a moment before or last month or twenty years ago. Sometimes I think I have merely been drawing a "self-portrait with fly rod," or the image of an aging fellow who frequently resembles a rather randomly tied fly, but this time, particularly in the last two sections of this book, I have tried to find more of what my professional life has amounted to than ever before and more of my personal life. Like Joyce's Gabriel, in "The Dead," I am often dismayed by what I find.

For fishing has only been a part of what has been a very full life, though an important part, a thing done for the bright joy of it, while studying, teaching, fathering, editing the work of others, writing about other matters, loving, being generally stuck up to my gills in the sweaty texture of life, never neat or predictable or pure; and like the boy in Roland Pertwee's "The River God," I have never for a moment been bored by it. Whether I've been diamond jigging from a boat drifting down the lower East River or pursuing finicky brown trout in a Western spring creek, fishing has always shocked my life with electrical intensity. I love it. Friends tell me my speech grows more animated when the subject turns to fishing; it has graced my life with adventure, mystery, challenge, the need for discipline, and fun.

This book is mostly about connections—to the fish, to the sport, to the ideas and books about fishing, to my professional life, and to my wife, whose drawings of my secret fishing life draw us, in our forty-first year together, even closer. If I veer from fishing to those other worlds, it may be because they are so intimately wed already.

In a sense, though, this book punctuates a long period of my life, begun in early childhood, refashioned as an adult with fly rod and feathered things, brought full circle by my having put it all, enough times now, to paper, each time, I think, circumscribing a larger circle around that deep core, my secret fishing life. I may or may not write much more about fishing. I have loved to write about it and, in myriad ways, what I have written has been exceedingly generous to me, offering me a

home for a thousand stories, memories, and even imaginings, and it has given me a score of far-flung friends.

Fishing has never palled, nor has my writing about it.

But increasingly now, in my sixty-sixth year, I feel tugged to fish in even riskier waters.

Nick Lyons
June 1998
New York City

I should not talk so much about myself if there were anybody else whom I knew as well. Unfortunately, I am confined to this theme by the narrowness of my experience.

—H. D. Thoreau
Walden

Part One

Seasonal and Spatial Matters

A FLY FISHER'S SPRING

In April, the season in my part of the world officially opens—and the season of preparations unofficially closes.

In February, I went to one of those shows—crammed with a fly fisher's candies—and bought four years' worth of sweets I'll never use. Then I arranged my 10,473 flies yet again— Eastern, early, mid, and late, Western, bass, bluegill, Northern saltwater, tarpon (will I ever go again?), spring creek, pike, and stuff-for-particularly-dumb-fish-of-many-species. I threw out a hundred, gave another hundred or so to Sandy, who will be fishing the East more this year. I suspect I have enough left. Maybe.

It wasn't such hard work. Each fly has a life all its own, with virtues that have proved their worth a hundred times to me— the sparkle shuck, the thorax winging, a certain color to the body and hackle—or flaws that make all other efforts futile. I am a fly addict and can pick and sort and chuck out flies for a week, nonstop, and then it's time to go on to my nineteen rods and thirteen reels, numbers down substantially because I'm always giving stuff away or trying to trade up.

This rarefication of our fly-fishing lives goes on, for better or worse, willy-nilly, for as long as we fish. It is flagrantly arbitrary, for a brilliant rod to one of us is a club to another—but we persist because of an absolute belief in our pursuit of the one good, true, and beautiful stick. My old friend Frank Mele, who died this past winter, searched endlessly for the perfect fly rod, but was too wise to settle for merely one—any more than he could ever settle for a single, perfect blue dun neck. Each neck had a luminous, evanescent color all its own, its own strength of hackle fibers, its own good and proper value for fly tying. He had fifty necks, each slightly different, as all blue dun—and all bamboo fly rods—can be.

The rarefication is an activity worth the doing. It takes with it a certain set of preferences for certain kinds of fishing experiences. At one time *any* fishing would satisfy me; I could fish all day with bait, lure, or fly, in almost any kind of water. I would fish any time of day, anywhere. With a full life and a lot of river under my waders, I find I just don't do that anymore. For one thing, I've learned this and that, and I'm less interested in fishing a Catskill river when the water is still forty-six degrees. I prefer to see a few flies on the water. And if it's early May, I'm inclined to think that midday and early afternoon will be best, just as I'll fish mornings and at dusk in the East when the summer heat has started.

You can't turn back. You've been in a good number of fishing situations, you've done a good deal, and you make a few choices. Sometimes I think that one of these days I'll rarefy my fly-fishing life flat down to bass-bugging on smallish ponds. I can't conceive of getting enough of that kind of fishing—but that may be because I've done too little of it.

A few well-worn fly lines needed to be replaced this year, reels cleaned, the tip top that mysteriously broke off in Montana replaced. I bought new waders and a fresh supply of leader tippet spools, which I change every year, and I sewed the two rips in my twenty-one-year-old vest. Why, I don't know, but I treated myself to a fourth pocket knife.

And then suddenly a new season started and I thought of Rilke's little poem about the spring having come again and the earth, like a little child, knowing many poems by heart. Along with the earth's green recollections of buds and sprouts, I began to remember too—a full fifty springs now, stretching back to my earlier days of fishing the East Branch of the Croton River on Opening Day with my friend Mort, when the rivers were always full of surprise and wonder. One year, improbably, I took a nineteen- and then a twenty-four-inch brown, both hook-jawed, both from the same pool on the Ten Mile River. On another, Tony almost got swept away in a heavy spring flood; now he's thirty-five, well over six feet, and quite big enough to save me from floods and hurricanes.

One day recently I tramped the muddy banks of a river I'd fished a couple dozen times in my youth. Here and there, remnants of ice and snow were tucked into cool, shady corners of the hillside. The earth had not yet remembered its buds or skunk cabbage shoots. The water was too cold; the air still did not have that hint of warmth that says "flies." I thought of a dozen friends I'd once fished the river with, now dead or in other parts of the world. Several were retired and did nothing but fish and play golf; their professional lives were over. One had given up fishing. I'd argued with another, Mike was dead, and I had to fight some days to remember his stories, the particular way he shook hands, smiled, cast a fly. The years had passed much too quickly and I couldn't even remember certain sections of the river; they were quite new to me—changed, no doubt, by floods.

Two weeks later, standing in a familiar run, I saw out of the corner of my eye a break on the surface. Looking closely, my head tilted to the surface, I could see a few Hendrickson shucks floating by, and a moment later, in the sky, I could see the reddish flies fluttering upward or aslant, to the trees. The swallows had seen them too and began their aerial dance above me, pausing just for a second to take one of the fleeting mayflies. Then there were a couple of fish rising, and I stood still for a moment, remembering, feeling quite happy with the sight. The river was coming alive, as I had seen rivers come alive a thousand times before. There was a spark of light on the surface, the bird sounds, the circles on the surface, the swooping birds. I tucked my rod under my arm, fetched out a box of early-season flies, found a Red Quill, and soon had my first fish of the new year. It was a bright brown, icy in my hands, not quite ten inches.

It is such a happy sight, the slight curl of a rising fish to your fly, after you have watched it float twenty times over a patch of water no more than two feet square, where you saw a fish come up. It is especially nice when it is the first trout of the season, for now, at their proper times—barring floods or too much cold or too much heat—all the Eastern hatches will start, in the tight schedule that makes April through June so irresistible.

There are places in the world where the season never ends, where you can fish throughout the year. Ted Leeson writes of such a place, his Oregon, in *The Habit of Rivers;* and others extend their fishing year by travel either south, southwest, or to the antipodes, Chile, Argentina. I hear the reports and I hear the sounds of pleasure in the voices. The fishing was different but superb. Bill caught a ten-pound bonefish in Belize, George a twelve-pound rainbow in a spring creek in South America. There are photographs to prove everything. It all sounds like fine sport. The photographs don't lie.

But more and more, I am framed by the Eastern season. When it ends, as late as October, I open my fish closet, pile in all the paraphernalia I've been messing around with since April, and close up shop for the year. I have other matters to attend to, other lives. And so everything sits until the dead of winter, when, by chance, I notice that there are a few less than one hundred days until April. "It's time to give serious thought to your tackle," Frank used to write me, and I always did and still do, thinking all the time, with increasing intensity, of the day when the first flies come, the true beginning of a fly fisher's spring.

GOING AND
COMING BACK

From those first days, at four or five, when I walked alone along the half-mile dirt trail from the hotel to the perch and pickerel lake, I felt that unique sensation of expectancy all fishermen feel when they head for water, always accompanied by a host of questions. Where on the big lake should I fish? Did I have the right hooks and enough of them? Had I forgotten my bobber, brought enough worms? Should I have left, as I'd planned, an hour earlier? Would I catch a pickerel even larger than the one I'd taken two weeks earlier?

And then, four hours later, returning from the lake, a pleasant tiredness in my muscles, my brain would wander very different paths—recalling, with the stark clarity of any recent disaster, the precise feel of that behemoth pickerel as it took the quarter-pound shiner I was hauling in, and the busting of the cheap bamboo stick that was my rod and then the busting of the line; recalling the oar I lost and spent twenty minutes retrieving when the wind came up; recalling another twenty minutes wrapping green cord around the part of the bamboo that had fractured and exploded. The rod had broken again, at the same spot, at the tug of a mere sunny, and, flustered, I'd dropped the worm box in the drink. And it began to rain thickly, and there was lightning that forced me off the lake, made me head briskly back to the hotel.

I'd caught some fish. I always caught some fish. I was born with some instinct for catching fish. But fishing was always a game that made you want more things to go right than wrong, where, at the right time, a lost fish could become a tragedy of the highest water. It's more so now, when I fly fish exclusively.

That same pattern repeats itself most of the times I go fishing—though the sensations have become marvelously more complex, even bewildering, and often enough related to other factors.

A friend who catches far more trout than most, all on the dry fly, says he never feels that the rich expectancy of a trip out is matched by any trip back, even after a pretty successful day. There are simply too many occasions for matters to go wrong on a trout stream: wind, rain, too much sun, no flies, a hitch in his casting, lost fish, high or low water, crowds camped at his favorite stretch, the fish simply not taking when he thought they should. His feelings almost always tilt, on trips back, toward what factors might have been better.

A literary friend, whom I did not know had the slightest interest in fly fishing, told me recently that he'd taken up the activity for about five years, to get away from his first wife. His trips out, he told me, were spectacular: the long day ahead of him, the prospect of wading to his thighs in a cool local river, the silence, the great peace that came for him on the water. He rarely caught a fish, and when he did it was irrelevant. But as soon as he stepped into the car to head home, he forgot the river, instantly, and a strange feeling of terror and trepidation swept through him like the vapors of the Angel of Death. I said that must have been pretty scary and asked him if he still had any interest in fishing. "No," he said, contemplatively. "I love my second wife and fishing reminds me of my first."

That all sounds pretty rotten, from whatever angle you look at it, but if you substitute a rugged, hectic life in a big corporation in a big gray city, and a middle-management job, you come to a place not too removed—at least as far as the fisherman is concerned.

Of course there are many of us, and I am now one of them, for whom a day on a trout river is so pleasant an event, such an amiable and engaging pastime, that it feels, both going and coming back, as comfortable as an old shoe. We go for the sheer joy of it, not to put notches on our rods. We go because no day on a trout stream lacks mystery, surprise, wonder, and suspense. We go for a glimpse of that most magical of sights— a spreading circle that is a rising trout. We see a world in that pocked surface. That spot becomes the condensed target for what we seek, the place at which—with all expectation—to cast our fly.

It's the same far and near, though I favor the shorter trip lately, even if it offers fewer and smaller fish. I like the immense surprise of catching a big fish in waters where you least expected it; I like to fish water I've fished a hundred times before, water that shares history with me, that I see in my head, going and coming back.

A friend knew a man who always paused at a bridge downstream from his parking spot on a remote New England river. He had seen, in his early fifties, what might have been the wavering tail of a truly gigantic brown trout, just twenty feet out, near the first abutment—though perhaps it was just weed, even a shadow. Still, each of the three or four times he fished the river every year, he stood quietly in the shadows and watched that three-foot patch of quieter water, just where the current glanced off the abutment and rushed toward the center of the run. The second year, in June, when the water was thinner and the sun at precisely the proper angle, he saw it with perfect clarity: a six- to eight-pound brown, perhaps twenty-six inches' worth, wavering, head upstream, high in the water, the largest trout he'd ever seen in an Eastern river.

He was a knowledgeable fly fisher and quickly saw that little blue-winged olives were coming down and that the big trout was probably taking either the nymphs just below the surface or duns with an indiscernible rise on the surface.

He waded a few feet into the heavy current between his shore and the lightly riffled water below the abutment and made a few tentative casts that at once convinced him he couldn't manage this maneuver. If he cast directly to where the trout was or even slightly upstream, the current caught the belly of the line so quickly that the fly dragged at once. He couldn't mend the curve in the line upstream fast enough, and he could not get directly above or below the fish, where he could work the much more manageable seam of lesser current, because he could simply not wade through the heavy current.

Trips to that river from then on were filled with the hopes that he would see that fish and hook it. He ran through new strategies in his mind; he read chapters in books devoted to this exact issue. He even tried the river in the doggiest days of summer. But he could not always see the fish and he never raised it.

The fish was there for two years, then disappeared, then was back. After ten years of going to the spot, of dreaming of it and of its auspicious denizen, he realized that he could not even pretend he was looking at the same fish. Surely the original brown, old when he first saw it, was dead, and its spot was always taken by an especially good fish, perhaps the best in the whole river, because the lower corner of the abutment gave a king plenty of food and plenty of protection.

The man never grew bored of the great fish, even of not catching it. Another ten years went by; he retired, some painful arthritis led him to fish less. But he only thought more about his great fish—the first one and its successors melding into one, transcending themselves, becoming some kind of emblem. He knew he could take the fish on a spinning lure or bait or perhaps a bead-head streamer. He had no special aversion of such methods, but they were not for this fish. He thought about the fish when he went to the river and then he fished a little or a lot for it, and then he thought about it every time he packed up his gear and headed home. His only disappointment came not from failing to catch the fish but from failing to see it, thinking then that his fish might have headed downriver with the last heavy rain, that one of the local kids had taken it by climbing down the abutment and fishing for it on a short line, with a heavy sinker and a live minnow. He saw it last July, big as a submarine.

This spring he called my friend and said he'd never fish again; he had one of the really bad cancers, and it was doing its nasty work like a swarm of red ants. He'd told his wife to call my friend when it happened. He wanted to be cremated. He wanted my friend to drop his ashes from the upstream part of the bridge.

"That fish gave me so much pleasure over the years—thinking about it, watching for it, pitching a fly toward that abutment. Every time I went I simmered with hope, and if I saw it, I returned radiant—otherwise, full of happy questions." He paused for a moment. "We were really linked, you know."

My friend said he did know.

"And now, since I couldn't have him, he can have me."

MESSING ABOUT IN
BOATS A LITTLE

More than a hundred pounds ago I rowed for the 150-pound crew at the University of Pennsylvania. We trained hard, carried the narrow racing shell to the Schuylkill River, grasped the long oars with both hands, and then swung hard when the little coxswain rhythmically barked commands through his midget bullhorn. There were fumbles and fallings-back; there was disharmony. But after a few moments we began to propel the boat with astonishing speed. Our bodies rocked forward and back as if controlled by metronome or prayer, our oars dipped lightly and in perfect unison, and we cut the surface so swiftly that I sometimes thought we were sailing inches above it.

After a moment, though, my arms began to tighten and I feared that what basketball skills I'd worked so hard to develop would be lost. Basketball was the game I loved most then, and played hardest, and since I'd already sacrificed my heart and grades for it, I gave up crew without looking back. Anyway, though I had always rowed, I had begun to realize that the

competitive rowing was not at all like the kind I did in an old
wooden or aluminum rowboat, on a lake, happily alternating
left and right strokes to my own rhythm, with my fishing gear
piled near the back seat.

For a while in my late teens (as the Water Rat tells the Mole
in *The Wind in the Willows*) I thought: "There is *nothing*—
absolutely nothing—half so much worth doing as simply messing about in boats." They isolated me from the world of land
and crowds and summer camp. They floated me. They gave me
more mobility than feet and better access to the water that I
was coming to love, that haunted my dreams. I liked nothing
better in the evening than to take out a rowboat by myself on
that Berkshire lake, head for a remote shoreline, and cast in
toward the bank, when the lake was glassy, even covered with
mist. And the rowboats were quite as comfortable as old shoes.

Canoes, at least for me, were for canoeing, but for fishing—
even in my lithe athletic days—they were too tippy. I needed
more solidity when I fished. I was never like those great fly
casters in the Winslow Homer watercolors or the husband and
wife (the wife with her baby in a papoose) I once watched on
Martha's Vineyard. The two paddled their canoe out of Menem-
sha Harbor into the choppy bay without a moment's hesitation,
to fish with flies for false albacore. It made my stomach shiver
to watch them, especially when the man stood and began to
throw a full eighty feet of line.

No, I prefer rowboats. I like their firm base, their respon-
siveness to both of my oars at once, the quickness with which
I can turn them, the precise (modest) speed with which I move
in them, so I miss nothing; and I love their reliable steadiness
when I've found a proper cove. When the wind is down, they
stay put. I can lean over and fuss with my big metal box crammed
with bass and panfish bugs. I can turn the boat slightly, running it parallel to the shore, and have a firm platform from
which to cast, a perfect angle to the shore. When I press the
long heavy rods I use for bass—10- or even 11-weight—into

motion and the heavy bug and line stretch out in front and then
behind me, I don't want to think of the craft that floats me; I
want to concern myself only with the business at hand—the
varied shoreline, that angled stump, the deadfalls, the lily pads
I'm working toward. I don't want my craft to tip when some
great buster of a bigmouth black bass crashes up and takes the
bug.

On the great rivers I've learned to enjoy the Mackenzie River
boats—especially when I get to stand in the prow, rod at the
ready, watching the shoreline that rushes past me and upriver.
My great impulse is to cast and cast—a demon in me. I want to
miss nothing. I want my fly on the water as much as possible.
Down it travels into one eddy, along the dark shadow beneath
the overhanging willows, into the strip of current that is the
feeding lane, behind that boulder, back again at the eddy behind
the boulder, as close to the rocky shoreline as possible. I manipulate the line so that the fly floats ten, fifteen, thirty feet,
drag free. I backcast once, maybe twice—no more. I bring the
line up backhand, then down. I watch, always, the white or
gray spot that is the fly as it slips downriver, drifting, dragging
for a moment, drifting again, is taken suddenly by a fish that
rises exactly where I expected it to be.

A good friend told me, when I floated the Beaverhead with
him, that I cast far too much, that I should cast only to a rising
fish, not to the good-looking water, of which there seemed no
end. If I kept doing what I did, he said, I just wouldn't be ready
when I actually saw my fish come up. He was right. Twice. But
I'm restless. I fish from a MacKenzie boat far too little, and too
many times there just aren't any fish coming up—though on
the Beaverhead there are more than on most rivers, especially
when Al Troth is rowing.

Having three thumbs, having graduated only recently from
my beloved Underwood Standard, Model "S," vintage 1945
typewriter to a 1950s Royal Standard, I do less well with motors
of all kinds than I'd like. I wish it were otherwise. They seem

like nifty ways to propel a boat in saltwater or on huge lakes. A flats boat in the right hands is a fine friend, ideally suited to its chores. Motored boats of all kinds are splendid tools for getting you out there and then back. I've used them on the huge St. Lawrence River, when nothing else was possible, and on some larger New England lakes, but they always make me nervous. My friend Mort, who has messed about in boats for most of his life, likes them, but twice when I've been out with him we've been towed back by another boat when a motor wouldn't turn over. No, give me a rowboat and oars every time, especially when I'm alone, and give them to me on a small lake rather than on a river, please.

The last time I went off on a river by myself was less than a joy. We borrowed Vaughan's Avon raft, the pontoon-like structure with a wooden section where we sat, and a couple of oars. The bottom was rubber and when we tried to stand we felt like we were on a waterbed.

"Have you done this before?" asked Vaughan, and I told him I had and that I had once rowed 150-pound crew. We were on the Madison and I realized only at the last moment, when I'd stopped boasting, that I had not come down this river by myself in fifteen years and fifty pounds. I wondered if the rubber could be punctured. If so, would the raft sink? I looked out across the river, thick with whitecaps from the afternoon wind, and thought that perhaps there was a better trip I could take someplace, someday. And then we pushed off, a couple of trusting friends and I, and the current immediately assumed command.

It took less than a minute, no longer, for me to realize that I had absolutely no idea of what I was doing. The boat moved too quickly, the wind took us wherever it pleased. I nearly killed my rear passenger when I slammed the raft into a mess of protruding willows on the far side of a sharp turn, and at the end—none too soon—I overshot the take-out spot by two hundred yards. Some fun. It wasn't my kind of adventure.

Call me old, call me fat, call me chicken—but I love best a simple rowboat on a small lake of some ten to twenty acres. I love it because I'm in control, because it's steady, because it gives me the exact access I want to a kind of fishing, increasingly, that I love.

At my age I can't think that I'll ever graduate—or degenerate—into a lover of brassy bass boats or even high-powered flats boats. As they say, some of my best friends love them. But I don't give up old pleasures, old clothes, old typewriters, old loves, or old rowboats without a struggle. Maybe it's my way of throwing a bit of sand in the careening machinery of progress; but I supect it's just that I've learned how happy I am messing around with what I know well, with what I'm comfortable. It's a challenge for a lot of us to be content.

4

DIAMOND JIGGING NEAR WALL STREET

Better fishing than you'd dream is nearer than you think. Put it this way: we stopped fishing before noon and a half hour later one of us was seeing a patient, another was having lunch with an old friend, and Gary was operating on some fellow's left foot. That's near. And if the fishing was not as rural as that on a mountain creek, it was very good fishing, indeed.

Dr. Ben Sherman of Brooklyn, who has four sons who are doctors and also passionate fishermen, called me late that night and said I had to try this fishing he'd been begging me to sample for a couple of years. I said I had no tackle ready; he said he'd have plenty of gear. It was too late for me to break a 12:30 lunch date; we'd be back in plenty of time for that. All I needed was to get to Exit 5 on the Belt Parkway in Brooklyn by 8:00. I wouldn't believe the fishing we'd have.

Here's what happened.

At 7:15, at West End Avenue and Eighty-fourth Street, I climbed into a cab, had a long conversation with an Iranian musicologist who specialized in historical Persian instruments, got lost in Brooklyn, and was at Exit 5 ten minutes early and on Ben's boat, with his son Gary and two friends, Dominick and Phil, a few minutes later. We were in Upper New York Bay, in the region of the Statue of Liberty, by 8:30—and ten minutes later I was astounded to see almost two feet of striped bass come over the side, get disengaged from a diamond jig, and then get tossed back. Dominick had done this pretty piece of business and he said: "I haven't seen you catch anything yet, Gary. Aren't they eating your bucktails this morning, Gary?" I gathered that Gary had caught most of the fish the day before, on bucktails, while the fish ignored Dominick's diamond jigs.

A few moments later Dominick had another; then Phil had one; then I heard Ben singing, "O, sweet mystery of life." He has a lovely baritone voice and it carried beautifully over New York harbor; he's the doctor for the Lafayette High School football team, along with much else, and I imagined him singing the same happy lines after touchdowns. He was singing with great enthusiasm as he cranked in a bass considerably larger than the twenty-four-inch limit.

Was old Nick doing it right? someone asked. I'd thought so. I'd been letting the diamond jig down to the bottom and then jiggling it a bit, then letting a few feet of line out, then jiggling the rod again. No, I wasn't quite doing it right. I was raising the rod too high on the upward jiggle and I was letting the tide lift the line off the bottom too far. The doctors agreed. Dominick agreed. Phil was busy catching another bass. There was an art to this jiggling business and I was far from mastering it; though I'd done my share of bottom bouncing when I was a kid, I'd long since lost my heart to a slender shaft of bamboo and a hatful of feathers, and my absorbtion in the complexity of such a love had wrecked any skill I'd had at bottom fishing. I had to reconcile myself at once to the sad fact that I made a poor jiggler of diamond jigs.

Gary did most of the boat work now and seemed content to let Dominick catch every fish in the bay. He was sighting on

Lady Liberty, all braced in scaffolding for repair and cleaning, and on a building among the many that rose like monoliths behind us, and on this and that, and he'd tool uptide, into a flock of birds, cut the motor, and then drift with the tide. The New York City skyline was majestic and looming; craft large and small kept horning us; the sonar showed black; and the five of us would drift downtide, our diamond jigs and bucktails working in the depths of Upper New York Bay.

I'm no fool: I kept watching Dominick. He was obviously a master of the diamond jig. I stood very close to him and watched him carefully and every few minutes (or less) he'd raise his stubby rod upward and would have (or have just lost) a fish. I knew the knack when I saw it.

Then I got one—a plump striper but under the size limit; then I got another, a little larger; then I got a bluefish, about five pounds; then Phil got a couple; then I heard Ben singing, "O, sweet mystery of life"—a half dozen times; then Dominick was at Gary again, every time he caught a fish, which was every few moments, and then Gary got a raft of them and there was no more ribbing, and every moment or so three or four of us would be doing a complicated bit of moveable chairs, going under and over, so as not to tangle lines, and Dominick got a truly big one and Ben was singing "O, sweet mystery of life" and telling me to take my time with the fish I had on, because there was a long winter ahead and I shouldn't rush things, so I didn't.

This happy business kept up for a couple of hours, without cease, and then I looked at my watch and saw it was 11:30. We'd never make it back to Brooklyn and from there back to my 12:30 lunch date in Chelsea, and anyway I had another blue-fish on and could not rush it.

I knew Gary had an appointment with a left foot and, while holding on to the blue for dear life, turned to ask his plans. This is to report that Dr. Gary Sherman was naked to the waist, in his jockey shorts, in full view of dozens of boats and investment

bankers from Wall Street buildings. He was silhouetted boldly against the World Trade Center and I rather wished I could get a picture of this, as he hoisted a dress shirt out of its plastic case, but my bluefish called, I turned and fought it for another five minutes, lost it abruptly, then turned back to Gary (whose father was singing that same happy song again) and saw Gary now fully dressed, with suit and tie in place.

We made one more drift, caught a couple more fish, and then scooted toward the South Street Seaport. On the way, through the rows of smaller buildings, I thought I caught a glimpse of Fraunce's Tavern, above which members of the Anglers' Club would already be gathering for some talk about last year's dry-fly fishing on the Beaverkill.

As we touched the pier, Gary marched up onto the hood of the boat, I said I might as well follow, and a few minutes later we were waving to Dominick, Phil, and Ben, who were going to make another drift and then head back to Brooklyn, where Ben had patients to see at 12:45. Since it was New York, no one but a few tourists even noticed the two of us climbing off the boat and marching past the chichi shops, chattering about the past three hours' work.

Gary said he'd be in the operating room in ten minutes. I hopped a cab and was fifteen minutes early for my lunch date on Twenty-third Street—but I stank a little, all day, from striped bass.

5

THE JUDGE'S SWIM POND

Irregularly, it was half the length of a football field, give or take an end zone, and narrow enough even for me to cast across. The Judge had built it forty years earlier for his kids to swim in. He'd put in a wooden dock on stilts, some bluegills, and a handful of bass. Now and then a neighbor added the last few minnows from his minnow bucket or a pickerel or a small trout from a creek across the hill. The trout were never seen again. All else flourished, especially the largemouths.

In the fifteeen years I drove upcountry to visit a close friend who lived nearby, I fished the Judge's swim pond a couple dozen times. I'd fallen in love with the long rod and poppers by then and always brought them along. We'd walk over from my friend's house after an early dinner on a hot summer evening with a fly rod each and a small plastic box with five or six poppers—panfish size to huge—and perhaps a few streamers and black leech patterns.

The pond was a complete, contained world—a cattail stand in the southern corner, a long bank with high grasses thick and snug to the shoreline, willows at the north end, the wooden dock that had buckled and leaned left, and a thirty-five foot strip of shore, sandy and sloping, where the Judge's family, for generations, swam. I heard the pond was fifteen feet deep in the center, which explains why the fish wintered over. There was a shallow flat near the cattails where the bluegills spawned in June, and in the shade under the overhanging willows, you could often find a big largemouth in August.

We'd always fish in the evening, from 7:30 or so right up until dark, and we liked the hottest of evenings best—the air thick with bugs, our shirts sweaty, the water flat, the fish eager for surface food. And we always caught fish—fat bluegills, unremarkable largemouths, pencil-thin pickerel that lunged at a leech or streamer, and now and then, when we least expected it, but most often when the sun was low and orange in the west, a largemouth that would break the surface as if a garbage can had been thrown in, a fish large enough to startle and make your heart pound, a glory fish, a hawg.

I loved the Judge's swim pond, perhaps because I came to know it so well, because it held such surprises, and because I shared it with a close friend. We chattered away as we walked to and from the pond, but we never talked much while we fished. We'd fall into that happy familiar pattern that only the oldest and best friends have, when half sentences, intonations, single words tell whole stories, especially when whispered across a quiet pond at dusk.

And then the Judge, whom I'd never met, died and his property was sold, and shortly afterward something that parallels death happened: my old friend and I had one of those ugly fights that only old friends can have—friends who know each other so well they know how to hurt each other most. We were big boys and ought to have known better, but we didn't, and then we did those things that are impossible to forgive and we have not spoken in ten years and never will.

Often as the winter wanes and summer dreams begin, I think of the Judge's swim pond and those evenings when the water was flat and bugs danced on its surface, when sweat dripped from the rim of my old fishing hat, when a popper pitched out and negotiated in could bring the energetic tugs of a bluegill or the eruption of a bass that would open eyes anywhere. I think of the pond and of the friend I once had and of the simple good times we had together and now never will again.

THE 193 MINUTES

Some wise fellow said in print that fishing was mostly expectation. We dream, we prepare, we tinker, we buy, we rearrange, we read, we go, and we wait; and what with the weather to delay us more and Al's cousin who needs to have his wind knots untangled every thirteen minutes, and an unexpected crowd at the Three Dollar Bridge, or last week's rainstorm, it's a wonder we ever get in enough fishing. Throughout it all, the planning and the doing, I have come to think that it's best done without clocks.

We do best when we simmer in our own juices, avoid the ticking clock—the handmaiden to our workday, and week, and year, to all programming, every deadline, all competition. We do best when we go slow and slower, when the going especially is caught up in its own time. And as we get older and wiser and surely more skillful, we can well expect our days to be more genial.

Last spring I was even busier than in most years recently; I didn't have time to plan, or much time to fish. In May, on a half hour's notice, I rushed upcountry, satisfied that I had arranged all that needed arranging after the close of the last season. I had made good order of my thousands of flies, putting each group in its own box, finding a box for every fly. Pale Morning Duns—in sizes No. 16, No. 17, No. 18, thorax, parachute, and Sparkle Dun—went into one of a dozen thin European boxes I'd decided would change my fishing life. There was room for a dozen little Olives, too, and enough Tricos for an emergency morning. I did the same with a couple of thousand other flies, blissfully, and the long gray November afternoon vanished. Under my new scheme, all the flies I owned of a given kind or for one use would go into their own box, which would hold an essential eighty to one hundred flies.

Some reels needed cleaning; one needed a new line, and I bought the most expensive one I could find. I fastened some braided butts to three lines and built four ten-foot leaders to attach to the butts. My rods were all right, but the only waders I could squirm into at my new weight had holes here and there. I gave away some extra nets, flies by the half-hundred, even a rod. Then, to assure myself that I was not becoming a minimalist, I bought two new rods—fast, downlocking, the newest graphite. Great stuff. I didn't need them, but I had every expectation of fishing more than usual this year; after all, I was pretty close to retiring from some bulk of my work, I thought, and that, finally, would give me time to fish in some endless summer of bliss.

In mid-May my old friend Sandy called one Saturday morning around ten o'clock and said: "You sure write about it a lot and talk about it all the time but I don't see you doing much trout fishing lately, N." He calls me "N." I told him he was surely correct but that I had a mountain of papers on my desk. Instead of retiring, I'd sort of reversed my ground at the last minute and gone back into the harness more than full-time. There was more paper in my life than ever.

"The paper will wait," he said.

"It grows when I don't weed it. Anyway, I owe it to my stock-holders to work."

"I happen to be one of your stockholders, and it's a perfect day and I'd like some company."

It was in fact a very tempting, muggy day after a late cold spring; there had been no heavy rain in more than a week. I'd had a few recent reports, all good.

So I grabbed the nearest rod and reel from my fish closet, fetched out four or five boxes marked "East—Early," "Large Dries—Eastern," "East—Later," slipped my vest and hat off their hook and into a carryall, and was downstairs waiting for Sandy in exactly seventeen minutes. He came four minutes later. We'd be back early but we'd have a few rejuvenative hours first.

I looked at my watch when we got to the river, then put it into the glove compartment. It was the most pleasant of mid-May afternoons—overcast, warm without summer heat, buggy; I'd have no need for clocks. There were a few insects around for most of the time we fished; I saw a couple of early Sulphurs and a half dozen March Browns within the first half hour. I used only big flies—mostly No. 10s and No. 12s—and it was a happy way to fish, flicking those high-floaters up into the head of little runs. I was happy that Sandy had gotten me out for the first time that year, and like Nick Adams in the Hemingway story, I wasn't going to rush my sensations. I fished slowly, and there was just the right amount of action. We leapfrogged or fished side by side, and Sandy caught most of the fish, which was all right.

Then I headed well upstream by myself, to a pool I knew that formed on the far side of the stream, beneath a small water-fall, against rock and a large bent hemlock. I had taken three fish, and it felt good to see the rise and feel the tug of decent fish against the curve of my rod. I was only upcountry for a day—a few hours really—and the fishing was superbly genial, restorative: exactly what I needed. There was a gentle quality to this Eastern fishing that, stuck on the West, I'd forgotten for a few years: the bright rush of a freestone creek, the pocket-water, the flats and ledge pools and choppy runs, the intimacy, the clarity of the water, the wall of hemlock overhanging the far bank. I'd taken a few fish; that was enough.

I approached the spot from well downstream. Planning carefully not to disturb the little pool, I blithely cast thirty feet across the gray stones. The line—my new line, not used before today, the caviar of lines—got hooked in a flotsam branch. I walked upriver to unsnag it, and then realized that I had not taken line back onto the reel. So it was tucked under some rocks, tangled in the branch, wrapped around one of my boots.

I probably should not have tried to roll-cast my way out of the problem in the first place, I thought, and certainly not three times, for now I saw clearly that the new line—dyed for me by Craig—was composed of a colossal bird's nest of knots, perhaps four or five related nests, twenty feet back, at my feet, around the branch. In fact, this was the mother of all knots, winding over, under, with little loops popping up here and there, with no beginning, no ending, no clear choice as to where to begin. I sat quietly on a rock, pecking away at it. I'd always fancied myself a pretty good knot unknotter.

But bad led to badder, tangle to worse tangle; more loops appeared, more routes seemed permanently blocked. From the edge of my vision, I saw a couple of those big juicy Sulphurs flutter over the hemlock pool and heard the splashy rise of a good fish. So I began to tug at the line and must now admit that I got very angry with it. The line simply refused to cooperate. I made some guttural sounds and then pulled it with both hands, hard as I could, to show I disapproved of the way my line was behaving. Then I took out my favorite serrated pocketknife and smoothly cut a fifteen-foot and a three-foot section out of the heart of my new fly line, tied all the loose ends together, clumsily, and tried to cast with the nasty knots. They caught in the guides, dropping my Sparkle-Dun Sulphur barely beyond my boots, then into the hemlocks. I took a step, tripped,

felt water enter my waders where the patch pulled loose, and dropped the contents of one very carefully filled fly box, with all my "Eastern—Later" flies, into the drink. The flies popped out and floated downstream—sixty to seventy of them—and the box twirled in an eddy and disappeared. The sky was ashen now, and I felt light rain on my face.

On my brisk walk downstream, I tripped twice more, pulled my bad hip out, saw the foot of my reel snap off, felt flat on my new graphite rod, and cut my face on a locust branch.

"You look like you've had quite a time, N," Sandy said when I came up to him. He had a good fish on. He was humming. He often hums when he has a good fish on, when he's enjoying himself.

I was breathing a bit too hard to say anything, or to hum.

He'd gotten nine fish, more than enough, and I'd just had enough. "Maybe," he said quietly as we walked back, "you ought to do this more . . ."

". . . stockholders," I mumbled.

". . . often. You're out of . . ."

It rained heavily before we got back to the car, where I slowly disengaged myself from my wet vest, my half-full waders, my wet shirt and pants, and broke down what was not broken of my rod. I didn't tell Sandy about my new line. Or my reel. Or how much my hip hurt.

In another few minutes we were in the car and the windshield wipers were rhythmically beating their tattoo against the wet glass. I put my hand in my pocket and realized I'd left my favorite knife on a rock. I retrieved my watch and looked at it. This sorry business had taken exactly 193 minutes.

7

LAST DAY

It's as easy for a fishing fanatic to let go of a season as it is to let go of a live electric wire. The last week of September I tried. I patiently oiled my reels and tucked them into chamois bags, clipped old leader stubs from my flies and placed each fly slowly back into its proper plastic box, packed away my trout rods, looked at it all, sighed, and locked everything safely in my fish closet until spring. I had been to Montana. I had caught more trout than I deserved. I had my memories. There is a time to fish and a time to live like a normal, rational, civilized adult.

But before I could lose the closet key, Larry Madison, a photographer and old friend, insisted we fish a bass lake near his home in Connecticut. "It has some truly huge bass," he said. I thought his offer over sensibly for three seconds. A last day in the country—to gird me for the long gray city winter—sounded harmless. Anyway, we'd be after bass and I'd long ago lost my heart to trout; there was no need to take any of this very seriously.

Larry did. He looked—walking ahead of me to the gray rowboat—loaded for bear. He carried a tiny spin-casting outfit, a bait-casting rig from which hung a five-inch swimming plug, and a gigantic glass fly rod he'd made himself, especially for big bass; it took a No. 10 or No. 11 fly line, he didn't remember which. I'd brought only a middling trout rod but I did not intend to fish intently; the day, after all, was an afterthought.

We took turns at the oars, the other casting in against the shore. It was a fishy little lake—maybe a mile around—with long gray trees fallen in from the shoreline, patches of lily pads and pickerelweed, beaver cuttings, stumps, marshes, and coves. The leaves of the maple, beech, and birch were umber, splashed with beige and red; an irregular V of wood ducks flew overhead. I could see no houses; there were no other boats. We had the lake to ourselves and might have been in Saskatchewan.

Before he'd made a dozen casts, Larry caught a two-pound bass on a bass bug of ridiculous size—perhaps three inches around. The bug was made of deer hair, dyed a dull orange, and had sprouts of hair at either end to make it look like a frog— a bullfrog, I thought—or maybe a duckling. Then he switched to the swimming plug, caught nothing, and then to the little spin-casting outfit and began to catch perch, one after the other, on a Mepps lure with a feather tail.

We came to a spot where the stream entered—sluggish in midautumn—and he said there would be pickerel near the drop-off of the sand bar. There were. The man knew everything worth knowing. I caught one on a popping bug, retrieved as fast as I could, and then he caught four or five on a spinner and a plastic-minnow combination. He is a superb fly fisherman and I advised him that he had sunk very low, indeed, but I wouldn't tell.

"Keep using that silly little rod," he said, "I'd rather keep catching fish." The pickerel were fourteen, maybe sixteen inches long. They'd take the lure in a lightning lunge and then, when we brought them in, squiggle like eels. I thought they'd be too bony to eat.

By 5:30 we'd fished three-quarters around the lake, had a fish box with twenty or so perch, pickerel, and that one bass sloshing around, and headed back toward the dock. The air was brisk. I started to tell Larry about Montana; he ignored Montana and said that this shore was good for truly big bass, six pounds or better, and that I ought to switch from my little toothpick now and fish with a real fly rod.

"That redwood?" I asked.

"If you want to catch a really big bass," he said.

So I tried his rod, with that ridiculous hair bug, but at first drove it too hard and the line buckled and fell in heavy loops.

"Let the rod do the work," he said.

I allowed the fly line to come back more slowly and then let the bend of the huge rod push it forward. Miraculously, I got more distance, great accuracy; I could learn to love a contraption that let me do that.

We slipped slowly down the shore, Larry rowing now while I cast in against the deadfalls, the stumps, the lily pads. I grew curiously more intent about this bass business. My arm worked in slow rhythms, the heavy yellow line rolled out, and fifty to sixty feet in against the shore I'd watch the big hair bug alight and then pop and sputter as I lowered the rod tip and tugged the line with my left hand. The lake was perfectly still: reflections of autumn color doubled the ruddy palette of the place. I felt increasingly mesmerized, intense. I wished Larry would stop alarming me with stories about the big bass he'd caught at night in August; he said he could have promised me a couple of big fish then. There ought to have been a fish there, and there, and near that tree angling into the water. I forgot Montana. I worked the bug with more care, intently.

The trees were dark silhouettes against the ash of the sky; the autumn air was sharp. A bat buzzed us twice and disappeared. Another ten minutes and this second season would be over for me. I did not want to let go of it now. I'd had a perfectly pleasant few hours, in the best of company, but now I was properly stuck on the image of these alleged six-pounders.

And then, not fifty yards upshore from the dock, my bug landed near a lily pad, lay still for a moment, I twitched it twice,

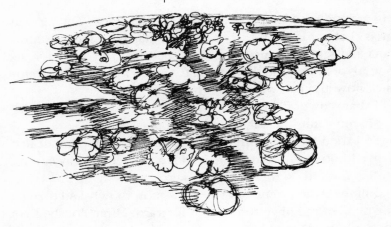

three times, and the lake burst up with a great rush and explosion of water and a largemouth bass half-rolled, half-jumped, its great green hump turning, the force of the thing heavy into the butt of the rod. I thought I'd been shot through with electric current. I thought someone had thrown in an anvil. And then it was over. The bug popped out of the water as sweetly as if it were a mayfly emerging from its nymphal shuck.

After a few moments I whispered, "What did I do wrong?"

"Not a thing. He slipped the hook is all. It happens. You look like you're in shock."

I couldn't even nod.

"That was a big bass—a very big bass," he said. "No. Don't cast again. He won't come back. Seasons end."

At his home, Larry filleted the pickerel, cut the backbone against the skin every quarter inch, soaked the fillets in milk, and then fried them all in hot oil. The bones vanished; the fillets were delicious. The great bass, its rise tremendous, its power still raising twitches and trembles in me during the long dark ride back to the city, would cook in my brain all winter.

Part Two

Theories and Speculations

8

ON THE TOP

There is an unsubstantiated story about my old friend Darrel Martin that he deliberately traveled to Croatia during that country's awful internecine war of several years ago because he believed that the fishing pressure on the great trout rivers there would then only be light. Well, he had one of them to himself and was having quite a fine time when a stern fellow in uniform appeared on the other side of the river and lowered a Uzi slung from his shoulder. The two men from different worlds looked at each other for a long while without speaking, bewildered, each trying to understand the weird moment, and then Darrel waved his hand, smiled, and said in slow, halting English: "It's all . . . right. Don't . . . worry. I'm fishing . . . a . . . *dry* fly."

Darrel neither confirms nor denies the event, but his lips broaden amiably when he is asked about it, for he well knows that whether it actually happened or not is almost beside the point: the story contains an inescapable truth, that the dry fly is in fact considered by many serious fly fishers to be superior to any subsurface fly—morally, logically, socially, even (perhaps) mystically. Why this should be so is another question, for the assumption that a fly that floats can possibly contain such qualities is both deep-rooted and absurd.

I am certainly not scholar enough to tell when it all began, no doubt before Frederic Halford, who codified the matter, nor how it progressed to its exclusive and elitist stature; but so serious an observer of our fly-fishing mores as the late Mr. Edward G. Zern once told me of a man who had been accused by his long-suffering wife, with good cause, of loving fly fishing more than he loved her. He did not hesitate, but immediately responded, "Wet fly or dry fly?"

The first trout I ever saw revealed itself to me when it rose to the surface of a small creek, pocking the flat roof of that watery world below me, causing the spreading circle that still never fails to animate my heart rate. I have pondered the mysterious electricity of that sight for nearly sixty years—and other sights that produce different effects. I have seen, with the help of Al Troth's great eyes, huge trout nymphing on the Beaverhead, and with the help of Jeffrey Cardenas's great eyes, schools of permit—their dorsals like the unrigged masts of ships—on the Marquesas flats. These are great sights. These are spectacular fish to fish for. These are memorable fish to hook and to battle, though I did neither. And I have fished a nymph to feeding trout in a carrier two feet deep, attached to a chalkstream in England, where the stalking, the presentation, the exactitude of it all must be every bit as demanding as fishing a dry fly to a fussy old brown trout feeding, in a three-foot indentation of a bank, on *Tricorythodes* eddying there.

I can think of a thousand difficult underwater situations—enigmas within the inner architecture of rivers—only a few of which I've been angler enough to master, and dozens of opportunities I had and refused, not from any sense that I'd fish a dry fly or nothing but because they looked too hard. I scarcely think a dry fly superior to a wet fly, or he who fishes it either a better or purer or higher-minded angler.

But that spreading circle on the surface, the rise of a trout, or the explosion of a black bass after a bug, remains a mystery that perplexes and taunts me. And so does the nagging question of why I find myself fishing the dry fly almost exclusively lately, losing a lot of good fishing time in the process . . . and losing a lot more catching.

I have a sincere desire to be neither a snob nor a supposed snob. No doubt I am an incompleat angler by my increasing preference—though I don't dictate to my brothers of the angle nor for one moment think myself their better. If anything, I am less able, less versatile, less capable of fishing to all the fishing opportunities available to me, more restricted—and clearly I catch far fewer fish.

What was so haunting about that trout rising in the little Catskill creek—and all the other trout I've seen rise? The fish was coming from its mysterious element—the world of water, beneath the surface of pellucid water—and touching mine, the world of air. So long as it moved beneath the surface—and I had watched it do so for twenty minutes—it was separate from me, in its own world; but when it touched the surface it entered mine.

I fished for largemouth bass a lot in my teens, on a dark lake in the foothills of the Berkshire Mountains. I fished for them with plastic worms, Flatfish, spinning lures like the C. P. Swing and the Mepps, live sunfish, newts, and several surface plugs like the Crazy Crawler and the Jitterbug. I'll bet both of those surface plugs are still marvelously effective. I can see them clearly from the height of fifty years, chugging their way from the dark surface beneath the overhanging pines, across the flat surface at dusk. I learned to fish those surface plugs in the evenings, when the lake was as still as the wind, in against the shore, exactly the way I now fish a bass bug—letting the thing sit, jiggling, teasing it, stutter-starting it, then making it perform a dozen little dances as it swims toward me in the boat.

I am hard put to find much appeal in what so many of the great bass pros do on television, jabbering away as they do so:

casting out and then retrieving an underwater lure with monoto-
nous regularity. When a bass hit a surface plug then, and when
one hits a bug for me now, I felt the same jolt of excitement—
simultaneously to eye and brain and hand—charging through me.

And then I found in the dry fly much of what I had been
searching for in fly fishing—the challenge of the exacting cast,
the need to master drag and thus be in active control of my
line at all times, the constant visual contact with the fly as it
floated downstream, the variety of ways the trout might rise
to my fly, the variety of instances that said we were connected.
I cannot think of a better comment on the dry fly than Ted
Leeson's observation that "the floating fly draws fishermen with
an ineluctable gravity, and the source of this attraction is not
difficult to locate. It originates with a flash, in the abrupt and
certain take of a trout. Few moments in fishing hold the same
immediacy and vividness as the rise to a floating fly, and none
are endowed with the same satisfying sense of closure."

The only possible practical argument for using the dry fly
more frequently is Lee Wulff's—that the dry fly fished on a floating line grants to the trout the sanctuary of its part of the river,
allowing the connection to take place only at that place where
air and water meet, and only at certain times. Of course this
also means that you can fish with a floating fly only at those
moments when the fish is likely to want its supper on the top,
and we've all heard that more than 90 percent of a trout's diet
is taken underwater. This confers upon the trout a lot of space
and time free from we who pursue it—and it limits our fishing.

But while it may limit the time we can fruitfully fish, it also
makes us a bit more observant, inevitably more interested in the
entomology of the rivers we fish. I know of three superb dry-fly
fishermen who fish only a few patterns, and those attractors like
the Adams or Hairwing Royal Coachman. I know of several who
once fished that way and have gradually begun to use some Latin,
because the Delaware or the Madison began to yield them a few
more fish when they learned which bugs were which.

Isn't one of the greatest pleasures of fly fishing that we can make it as simple or complex as we choose? And the choice, to fish an artificial fly that imitates an insect upon which a trout is feeding, to pitch our fly to a specific feeding fish—even as a straight-pool player must call his pocket, not merely bang away—is an honorable game, one that demands a bit more of us and therefore gives more. More and more I prefer that game myself.

I like the big bug that may imitate a frog or mouse or duckling or less determinate stew, resting near the lily pads at dusk, twitching a bit from its nervousness, then disappearing in a great washtub of a rise; I like the slashing strike of a rainbow that you can see lurching several feet through the heavy riffles on the Madison for your fake salmon fly; I like trout in a fixed feeding lane on a Catskill river, lunching on Hendricksons that float down on a cool gray late-April afternoon like little sailboats; and I cannot resist fishing to a shy trout on a river like the Firehole, the fish slipping so gently along the far bank, below the grasses, that you can just hear it thinking its lips against the surface can betray it.

Mostly, and perhaps solely, I love to fish on the top because something in me responds to the rise, loves the experience of sight as much as touch, and more so because I must concentrate unblinkingly and intently—and because it's just so much fun.

9

NUMBERS CHANGE

There is a photograph of me taken in our backyard in Brooklyn nearly fifty years ago. I am wearing the man's felt hat that I always wore on fishing trips in my teens, holding a rod in my left hand, kneeling behind my wicker creel. On top of the creel are five small trout—silvery fish, impossible to tell if brook, brown, or rainbow, all stockers. On the ground in front of the creel are five of what we called "holdovers," fish that had been stocked a year or two earlier and had survived; there were no wild fish in the rivers we fished. The holdovers are fat browns, seventeen to nineteen inches in length, and even in the faded print their spots show sharply; we valued these much higher than the others, not merely for their size. The rod I am holding has a spinning reel at its base. This is serious business and I am not smiling.

Our state limit in the late 1940s was ten trout and "limiting out" was always our goal. We did it whenever we could. It provided a yardstick against which to measure our skill, and the day. Limiting out by eight in the morning was better than doing so by five in the afternoon. After we reached ten we stopped fishing and rooted for our pals. The limit was set by the state and we never questioned our right to take what we were allowed.

There are much larger catches in angling history—recorded with unquestioning pride in numbers. Consider these bloody portraits of Thomas Tod Stoddart, a popular nineteenth-century writer:

> [Mr. Stoddart] was literally *clad* with salmon and sea-trout; his large hamper was full, and five or six strapped on his rod hanging across his shoulder and down his back, the perspiration streaming down his face and dripping off his beard and hair.

When told that he's killing himself with such a load, he says: "I'm doing this to let the beggars see that all fishers are not liars." Or this:

> His basket [a very large salmon one] was filled, aye, *crammed* with trout. The weight could not be less than a quarter of a hundredweight and nearly as many were lying on the bank, which he had begun to strap up on a strong cord. 'Man,' he says, 'if I had not been out of bait, I could have killed as many more.'"

In our late teens, some of us began to throw fish back, heeding Lee Wulff's wise call that a gamefish was too valuable to be caught only once; we did this before it became popular and in the watersheds we fished our gesture was greeted with hoots and wry smiles. But keeping fewer fish did not mean we caught fewer. In fact, we caught more. Our skills had improved, our passion multiplied, and now our satisfaction came in numbers caught. "Sixty-two browns, fourteen to twenty-one inches," a friend boasted after a trip some years ago. Forty-eight, fifty-one, thirty-seven. Sometimes the numbers were physically impossible

—did those friends cast, hook, land, and release a fish every sixty-seven seconds? Did their numbers include short strikes and inspection rises? As throwing back fish has taken on a moral height only slightly below sainthood, mendacity has grown like crabgrass.

I stopped killing most fish after I was part of a wholesale fish slaughter, with spinning rods, in my early twenties. Huge trout were in the spring-fed cove of a Western lake and I caught twenty or thirty of them, big fish, bigger than any trout I'd then seen, and killed them all, hooking my thumb under the upper jaw and breaking their necks, to give to some local loggers who wanted them for a fish fry. By dark, my thumb was raw and bloody and I could not catch another. I'd had my fill of it, I felt guilty, and it had grown not only gruesome but boring. Some change began in me that evening at the lake—when the miracle of big fish and the numbers of them and the killing of them began to pall; but it was not merely a reaction or the taking on of a conscious ethic.

A dozen years ago I began to fish a pool that at first frustrated my best efforts. I had shifted most of my fishing to the fly rod and had learned it reasonably well, but not well enough for this tough river. I first fished this pool from the wrong position, with the wrong flies; I lined the fish, stood up and made the whole pool go dead for an hour, underestimated the head of wild fish it held. Once, standing, with the light at just the right angle to the water, I saw down into the deepest portion of the pool, just below the riffled bend, where the water slowed and broadened. Fluttering near the bottom like so many frightened minnows in a pail were forty or fifty wild browns, from near-fingerlings to fish of up to twenty-four or more inches. They'd chosen this spot because the fecund riffle provided them with a maximum amount of food and the depth gave them protection from predatory birds, their worst enemies.

I didn't catch a fish the first year, caught a few by chance the second, and eventually became master of the pool. The key lay in matters that I learned by trial and hundreds of errors. I had to sit rather than crouch or kneel, which kept me low all of the time and comfortable enough to wait for precisely the right moment to cast; and there was indeed a right moment, determined by when a fish had last risen and how frequently it was coming up. I had to inch my way along the bank so that I came close enough to the fish that I could make the shortest possible cast—no more than twenty-five feet; I had regularly, at first, tried to cast forty-five feet or more, from below the pool, over braided currents, and over what I had learned were dozens of skittery trout. From my new position, and with a short low cast, I never lined the vast number of fish in the belly of the pool but fished directly to those in the bend-riffle. I lengthened my leader to twenty-two feet. I discovered that the trout would take no high-floating, Catskill-style dry flies but would come to emergers and those that, without underhackle, lay flat on the surface. Two or three patterns worked best and I depended upon them—but I had four or five others that alone proved fruitful at times.

I used a No. 4 rather than a No. 5 rod and line for this pool eventually, and brought a little net with a long handle so I could trap flies circling into the eddies near my feet without moving. If I did not stand to play a fish, despite all the splashing as I brought one to hand, another fish or two would begin to rise within ten minutes. And when all of this came together, I could take eight or nine large wild fish from this pool without budging.

Five summers ago I came to the pool one day about 11:00, when I knew several mayflies and a small brown caddis would be on the water, shimmied into my familiar spot, and looked at the riffle. A fish was bulging in the current. I scooped up some insects, found a lot of Pale Morning Dun spinners, watched a bit longer, and then made my old short cast up into the riffle. On the third cast, the fish took. It proved a fine brown and after I released it I sat quietly, fluffing my fly, taking fresh line off the reel for my next cast. In ten minutes a new fish was up—did they issue meal tickets here?—and it took the first fly I pitched upstream, one of Craig Mathews' No. 18 Pale Morning Dun spinners, with bits of Z-lon for wings.

I knew this could be a remarkable day. I might break my record of nine fish at one sitting. There were flies everywhere now, even a few Green Drakes, and within a few minutes two more fish were feeding.

There is an old maxim that a fly fisherman should never leave a feeding fish—since you never know when you'll find this one, or a number of them, up again—and I did not leave the pool. But I also did not make another cast. I watched. What a deliciously pleasant sight—two, perhaps three good fish high in the water, dorsals out, wolfing down fly after fly. I was a long distance from those waterways close to the city, to which I'd trekked every spring in my teens, fishing overfished water, keeping everything I caught. We had *needed* those catches then, for our self-esteem, our competition with friends, an indefinable urge, always, for *more.* Now, plying a craft that had taken so much time to learn well, with subtler tackle, did I still have numbers on my brain—numbers that translated into a certain quantity of released fish in some state of exhaustion,

even shock, with some immediate fallout from hook and fight? Was it enough to know that I *could* now take a half dozen or more trout from this once-difficult pool—if I so chose?

The flies slowed an hour later and then there was only one last fish up, taking everything, wantonly, a pushover. It had been a wondrous hour and, without making a conscious decision, I realized that I just did not want to stick a hook in any more fish that day; two, coupled with all I'd seen and learned, made a lovely, intense, successful morning.

Five years have passed and I've fished that honey hole a dozen times since. I like to kill an occasional trout now and then these days and to prepare my catch carefully and eat it. I'd forgotten the special pleasure of this whole process for too many years; in the right rivers, it hurts not at all to do this. But I never kill fish from this pool. It glad it's still there. I'm glad it's as fecund as it ever was. I'd glad it's always a bit different, and I find that those slight variations in its contours and the feeding patterns of the fish on a given day make it even more exciting to return to this place that I've mastered than I'd have expected.

I've always gone to rivers to catch fish, and I always will; that will remain my primary reason for going. Only the source of my pleasure—and the numbers—have changed.

10

BAD SPORT

I once wrote a story about a sailfish-fishing trip on which I had almost been conned by a chiseling charter-boat captain into some extravagant extra costs. It was accepted by a novice outdoor editor—skillful but fresh from another field—and then, when he was sacked, the story never appeared. I was told by the new editor that he'd tried hard to find a "*good* charter" story to balance it, each beginning on a facing page, but couldn't. Finally (though I had been paid for the thing) it was returned. I promptly sent it to two other national magazines and both promptly rejected it as "having too low a view of sport"; then John Merwin published it and there were no complaints.

I've always been troubled by the rejections—that is, the reasons for them. Too low a view of sport? Good grief: those magazines had been publishing puffery for decades. The problem came back to me a few weeks ago when a young friend had a fine article rejected, which I'd submitted for him, because it had "too many no-nos" in it. The no-nos were moments when the hallowed world of sport was less than sportsmanlike. "I'd better *not* write that piece about the time, when I was seventeen, I shot a grouse on the ground after a frustrating day," the young man told me.

All this is a sad, unfortunate feature of many outdoor magazines: they try too hard to depict the sporting life as idyllic, filled with honorable square-jawed men, embodying the purest, most puritanic code of ethics. I don't know whether they do it to support their advertisers, because they think their readers want only sunshine and light, or because they've acquired a few bad habits, like prudery. Though I fish far less than I'd like, I've not found such a world to exist out there. Nor does anyone else really think it does.

All guides are not legendary. I gave my fly rod to one who had been instructing me a bit too tenaciously all one week and it was clear from his first cast that he'd never fished a fly before. I had another who put me at the tail of a fine pool out West, to fish a dry fly upstream, and then got in at the head and fished a streamer—quite vigorously—down so close to me that our flies hooked. It was a day of ferocious emotions. He kept up a loud and tireless tirade against "Eastern dudes and experts" who thought they knew how to fish. I practically cried with laughter when his graphite rod—an early model—exploded during a double haul. And then, against all odds, and not particularly trying to do so, I had a bit of spectacular luck and caught fish after fish, up to better than twenty inches, for three hours. The trout were on hoppers and my lousy casting didn't show.

Would anyone have published such a story?

I don't think so. They'd have been worried about the guides who advertise; about the thousand readers who would write in about their great guides—and I've had many; and about the "low view of sport" the story depicted.

But there's worse out there. I have been in all too many fishing camps where every other joke was racist, anti-Semitic, at the expense of women or children or modern art or any art or anyone or anything "beneath" the sports, where the talk was coarse and competition corrosive, where adultery was praised as the "supreme adult activity" and philandering, rather than fly fishing, was the dominant sport.

To report these things is not to say that I liked them or participated in them, or that, in writing about them, I in some way endorse them; nor does it say that I want to take a moralistic view about them; nor does it say that I have not had idyllic days and days when I felt some of the best in me and those around me brought forth by the sport we loved. But those moments of "bad sport" were there, and any depiction of the outdoors ought someplace, now and then, to show that sportsmen—even fly fishermen—ain't a whole lot more perfect than a whole lot of other people.

What troubles me most is the cover-up.

Why must magazines—and a lot of holier-than-thou boosters of sport—depict it in a sentimental, whitewashed way?

Readers are sometimes as much to blame for this as editors. There was some harmless passing of gas in a notorious story some years ago and the volume and tone of the responses was something wonderful to hear. I'm not sure why. Was it out of place in the sweet drawing rooms of sport? Was it in bad taste, "uncouth"? Did it spoil the illusion? Must I mention that one of the finest stories of the twentieth century, "My First Goose" by Isaac Babel, has a perfectly splendid farting scene, to justify the presence of a little gas in a fishing or hunting story? I doubt if writing about fly fishing will ever have the remotest chance of attaining the level of art unless it contends—as art does—with everything out there, fish, flesh, and foul.

That's the irony. I want the level *higher,* not lower. I'm not particularly pleading for more gas in fly-fishing stories, or more lousy guides, only that they be there when they're needed, for good and proper aesthetic reasons. "Fair and foul are near of kin/And fair needs foul," says Crazy Jane in a W. B. Yeats poem. Of course it does. Anyone who takes the prose of sport seriously, who wants it to register the activity most sensitively and lastingly—and truthfully—must finally come to such a position.

Otherwise, what we read—and some of us write—will only be governed by silly, frustrating, and ultimately perfumed illusions.

11

JOURNAL ENTRIES

Like my old friend Clyde, I keep a fly-fishing diary and fill it with random observations about our odd passion; often I read these over in the winter, when my head is active and my boots dry. Some of them seem complete enough in themselves not to be shoehorned into some other form. Anyway, they are generally all I have to say on the subjects.

In Short Praise of the Royal Coachman

I got my first one from an old Army buddy, who used the bright red, green, and white fly exclusively. And I always caught fish on it—in New Jersey, the Catskills, the West—and always went back to it in tough times.

Preston Jennings thought it imitated an ant or an *Isonychia;* but I'm convinced now that its breadth of fish-catching ability proves something else: it imitates no living thing and therefore is never regional or time-sensitive, like a March Brown or Pale Morning Dun, which work primarily when those flies are hatch-ing. Frankly, I have no idea why it catches so many fish—except perhaps because we can see it so well. Several times lately, in my increasing zeal for matching real stuff, I've thought of retiring it, like a club retires its best scorer's number. But I won't—not as long as it remains as irresistible to trout as a bonbon to a boy.

Roads

Superhighways have made the distant near, the inaccessible available to all. We get everywhere faster today. A river I know that was two hours from my apartment is now a little over an hour. This better access all seems very convenient until we consider the corollary: roads are the harbingers of crowds. There was a section of a nearby creek that kept its appeal for me precisely because even though the crowds on the main section increased, few people would make the effort to walk two miles down an increasingly difficult path to the productive lower section, which I had mostly to myself. The extra effort meant better fishing, and I'd earned it.

On Opening Day this year I took a friend on that trek. When we got there he asked if such a walk was really necessary and I assured him that it was. Then why, he asked, was that couple strolling up the new mud road that entered from another direction?

Like a Miser

We all know that great old fish grow exceptionally wary. I have seen them with a nose just poking from beneath a safe under-cut bank, hovering at the very bottom of a pool, below lesser brethren, coming out to play only under cover of a gray day, nightfall, an exceptional hatch of a large fly or grasshoppers in the field. Hewitt Wheatly (in *The Rod and Line*, 1847) said it best when he described one such fish: "He had been hooked two or three times and was consequently as wary as a miser, when his son begins to beat about the bush, introductory to some pecuniary hint."

Our Brand of Tragedy

Nothing quite matches the frustration of losing a large fish, and nothing has a greater tragic aura, in miniature, than a slipped knot. Like all great tragedies, from Oedipus to Lear, one's downfall is caused not by some malevolent demon in the universe but by our very own tragic flaw. In this case the tragic flaw is impatience.

The Unexpected Strike

We like to think that our triumphs proceed from pure skill— that our mastery of the quadruple-haul cast, adding an average minimum of seventeen feet, six inches to our casts, directly caused our last great catch. Sometimes, in fact, that is so. But why have I caught almost as many fish trailing my line in the water, rapidly retrieving a sunken dry fly, on a collapsed backcast, when the wind took my fly into left field?

Frankenstein Trout

News reached me recently of genetically engineered rainbow trout that resist whirling disease; grow at a rate 4.3 times that of natural rainbows; can withstand heat, cold, and pollution; attain sizes of 15 pounds and up; and can bite through all but the new superalloy hooks made in Silicon Valley. This sounded nifty to me, except for the part about nibbling through leather wading boots to get to toes.

"Economics will decide whether or not to develop the breed further," said Professor L. D. Daggett of Utah. "If fly fishermen want transgenic trout and are willing to pay for them, watch out!"

For myself, I know a pond that has four-inch wild brookies, pretty as jewels. That's the size they grow in that environment. I find them irresistibly lovely, and they don't nibble toes.

Mr. Stonefly

I told Mari that Mr. Stonefly had been reported fifteen miles upriver, and that even a flailer like me could catch trout at such a time. "I'd like to see that," Mari said eagerly, so we set out, and along with dozens of giant stoneflies in the willows, I counted sixty-one cars at the bridge, on both sides of the river. I didn't bother to ask any of my brothers of the angle what was cooking but scooted another five miles upriver to a nice spot I knew on the open plain. "Wasn't the bridge a good spot?" Mari asked. "Everyone else seemed to think so."

At the new spot, where I'd fished twenty-five times alone, was a new house. The spur road that led directly to the river had rocks across it, but no sign, so I just drove around them. I made exactly seven casts. During that period eleven drift boats floated by. I turned to head back to the car after a ferocious afternoon wind came up. It was followed by rapid darkness, then streaks of lightning and pelting rain. I threw my gear into the back of the car and jumped into the driver's seat, panting. Mari was there. She said, "I thought you said even you couldn't miss when Mr. Stonefly arrived."

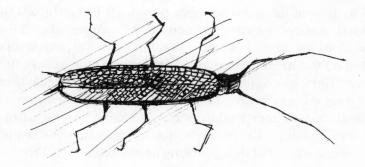

The Price of Truth

I was coming off the Madison after a two-whitefish morning and met a robust man suiting up. With him were his two blond daughters, perhaps six and seven. "How'd you make out?" the man asked, and I told him truthfully about my two fish; I did not mention that one was the biggest of its breed I'd ever seen. "Funny," he said, shaking his head in disbelief. "The stonefly's on and it shoulda been hot this morning. I got two four-pound browns yesterday afternoon on a Sofa Pillow, twenty-two inches apiece, like twins." He took out a tape measure, if not to prove anything then at least to rub it in.

I turned to the daughter nearest me and, without thinking of possible consequences, asked if this was a big old fib. The girl was so shocked that I might consider her daddy a dirty liar that she gnashed her teeth and might have bitten me if I hadn't made a hasty exit.

Sour Trout

I recently heard of a club that thought it could raise money for its stocking program by taking out life insurance on its most unpopular member.

Etiquette

As fly fishing has become more popular it has attracted the widest possible spectrum of people. As an egalitarian, I find this all to the good. I like diversity. But I don't especially like, on or off the stream, those folks in the world who believe they have "The Right of Rip-off"—and I especially don't like them on waters we all share. Take those three young men on the Gallatin last summer, flailing away, beating the water to a froth, bored silly with it all, dressed to the nines in the newest stuff, horsing around, and then plucking flattish stones from the bed of the river and calmly skipping them across the run I was fishing.

Color Theory

My friend Clyde, always a man far in advance of the crowd, has been thinking about color. So he studied (1) the nature of light; (2) the nature of those substances that reflect light, with their own textures and hues; (3) the nature of our eye—and the trout's eye. He read Christian Huygen's *Traité de la Lumière,* which proposed that light was "wave motion"—and Clyde preferred this to Newton's Corpuscular Theory. He then went on to Max Planck's Quantum Theory, Richard Feynman, Harding, Marinaro, Einstein, Jennings's unpublished "iris" theories of color in salmon flies, and Datus Proper, who thought color far less important than size and shape. He bought Italian vises and Spanish cocks to improve his tying, studied iridescence—in peacock herl, Antron, and Sparkle Yarn—and only gave up all of his studies and went back to using an Adams exclusively when he hit a stone wall: the purple plastic worm.

12

TRUTH IN
OUTDOOR WRITING

An outraged fellow wrote to me once, claiming that I had done as much to ruin a river he'd fished for years as those who used motorboats and chain saws on it. The boats, he said, cut up the shallows pretty badly, and what they didn't cut up, the boaters cut off, with saws—those deadfalls, overhanging brush and branches, and logjams we all know are so compellingly trouty. Those folks didn't sound like good company.

Since in my own steady way I've rather tried to save rivers for the past thirty-five years, and since I share the man's distaste for motors and saws near trout rivers, I wasn't sure whether to cheer him on or swiftly kick him in the kidneys—for I'd spent months on that article, trying to get it just right, and I take words to be both pointed and potent.

I've many times kept the true name of a river or lake out of what I write—a limestone bluegill lake that produced fish bigger than many frying pans; a spring creek with soft banks that crowds would decimate; a two-acre pond I rather selfishly wanted for myself, as long as I kept it an old fisherman's little secret; some rivers being "loved to death," as my friend Steve Meyers fears has happened to the San Juan. Friends tell me I have an obligation to readers to report accurately and with names and details on what I've had the privilege of seeing and fishing; my outraged reader said it was the curse of all outdoor writers, apparently, that they named names. I don't know. Naming or not naming just isn't the job I shipped for; sometimes you do, sometimes not. It's the river on the page, I've convinced myself, that matters most—the "imaginary" river with real trout in it.

The river I had written about was the one Hemingway used as the rough prototype for his fine story "Big Two-Hearted River." Somehow that was still a secret in 1957, when I was a graduate student at the University of Michigan and first fished it, above the undisguised town of Seney. I reported my findings, with some elation, to Professor Sheridan Baker, with whom I had a class. Baker's eyes widened and he said he'd just finished an article but not yet published his discovery. His article was the first to announce what was so obvious it was even overlooked by Jack, Hemingway's son, when he camped on a river thirty-five miles northeast of Seney, called the Big Two-Heart. Baker's article is still one of the best on Hemingway's story.

In the 1950s and thereafter, the river had its threats, not from its reputation as a literary shrine, but from too many boats, too much casual use, too many chain saws, too much bait fishing. A Michigan friend said it became "everybody's toy." Ted and Jerry and half a dozen other friends had made a pilgrimage to the river, as I first did, and most had merely looked for a few hours, paid their homage, got bit by some legendary mosquitoes, and left. We were no threat. People who love a river and its history rarely treat it like a hotel bath towel. What they take from it is a lot lighter (and more serious and durable) fare than a sackful of trout.

Hemingway, who snipes at fly fishers in his story, claiming they left flotillas of thrown-back, damaged trout in their wakes, much preferred to kill than to return; he caught with his friends, by his account, more than two hundred brookies on the trip that formed the basis for his famous story. He scarcely tried to hide the name of the river he fished, though my late friend John Voelker always insisted he just wasn't a "kiss and tell" fisherman. It was fiction, after all, and in the best of the genre everything gets changed that (for the needs of the story) needs to be changed. You put a swamp where you want one; you take a hollowed-out log from a creek you fished ten years earlier; if you're lucky, you don't have to tell stretchers about the size of the fish. Hemingway said quite bluntly about his story, a number of times, "I made it all up." He didn't make up the Soo, the Morro, a dozen restaurants that his aficionados dine at seventy years later, nor much else in his nonfiction; he never especially tried to protect them—only to let his readers know of his wise judgment in such matters.

He called his dark story "Black River" first, after the name of a downstate river that he liked to fish. "Big Two-Hearted" is better—a big river with two hearts, larger in spirit than most, mysterious, perhaps with oxymoronic hearts. He could easily have changed the name of the town, Seney, if he'd wanted to protect the fishing. I don't think he gave such matters a thought; the burned-out Seney, its volatile history, the black grasshoppers, were just what he needed. His character, Nick, was burned out, too. The real swamps helped.

The river isn't my kind of fly-fishing river. It's overrun and overhung with tag alders so that you can barely cast in most of the water, unless from a boat. And it's really too small a river for a boat, and they shouldn't be allowed on it. The water's mostly too deep for good dry-fly fishing, which happens to be what I like best. It's best fished with a live minnow, worms, perhaps the grasshoppers Hemingway used, or a lure that flutters and spins when retrieved. I'd have loved such a river in my teens.

After a couple of sluggish days, I asked the proprietor of the local catchall shop for some suggestions, and he told me—head

tilted to be sure that no one else in the empty shop would
hear—that a Panther Martin spinning lure, with half a worm
trailing it, could be deadly. I have only fly fished for the past
forty-five years, but I remembered the famous maxim "Once
an artist, twice a pervert," and decided to give this rig a try. I
blithely bought a spinning rod and other necessary weapons.
In the interest of truth and without fear of confessing my deepest sins in public, I admit to doing so.

My outraged reader leapt upon that revelation, that truth,
with immense glee: ah, a dedicated fly fisher using a spinning
rod, as if by the very nature of the act I had damned myself
eternally, without chance ever of reprieve.

In the course of my unforgivable sin, I caught and released
a few small brookies on the silly rig and had one truly large trout
flash for it . . . and miss. I reported all that, too, honestly, and
it seemed clear to me that I had not hurt the fishery by such
activity or by the words I'd used to describe my actions.

It's not the mention of its name that hurts a river—and I had not exaggerated the slender success I'd had. Writers hurt a river by being its shill, its exploiter. And rivers are ruined long before they're written about, through poor management, overuse, poor fishing habits that deplete its stock, clear-cutting, damming, bank erosion, overstocking, motorboating, the introduction of ailments like whirling disease, and oh, a thousand other crimes. You take too many fish and they won't be there. You allow boats to cut up the beds and the trout won't spawn. You destroy cover and the trout will have no sanctuary and will surely light out for the next county. You overstock and bad trout, as Gresham's law has it, will drive out the good.

Conversely, you put no-kill regulations on a substantial part of a river, and the average size of the fish and their numbers will surely grow throughout the entire watershed. Since the pleasure in fly fishing is probably as much in the doing of the thing and the catching rather than in the killing, fly-fishing-only regulations can only help. The point is to protect the river, so that there will be *some* resource for a variety of different people who want to use it. Those gestures that increase the fecundity of a river help everyone; open regulations, despite the implication of their name, help those who want to take more from it. Moderation, thoughtfulness, intelligent use of a resource— all this sort of jazz is absolutely needed in our time.

But who will do it? And how?

I suspect a river needs friends to protect it—a dedicated band of serious fishermen who understand the history of a river, who have studied its biology and thought deeply about how to manage it, who respect what the river once was and what it might be, who want to protect it. Words can help. Public words are often the only way to galvanize such support. And the words need not only be the strident, if well-meaning, shouts of outrage, but the words of affection and understanding. If ever a river has needed a few more, not fewer friends, that one is it.

13

ME, TOO

Not long after my old pal Clyde was informed that there was very big money to be made writing fly-fishing books, our longtime friendship almost headed south. His longer studies of the fishing neurosis, his extensive and esoteric notebooks, his postmodernist piscatorial poetry had sadly earned him only enough money to buy a couple of jars of salmon eggs. "My new concept," he told me, "is to tell the folks how to catch ten times what they're now catching on flies, of whatever species—and who knows more about catching fish than I do?—and make a small fortune."

He was surely right that, for forty-five years, he'd always caught ten or more times the number of fish I caught, and he knew, of course, that I ran a small publishing firm that published some fly-fishing books. He said that for a mere couple-of-hundred-thousand-dollar advance against future royalties, he could make me a huge fortune.

I told him I only wanted to be thin, not rich.

"But there are ten million fly fishers, all just waiting eagerly for my—"

"Happily there aren't ten million fly fishers," I told him so-berly. "The number is extrapolated by the Internal Revenue Service from the bald fact that eight hundred and twenty seven thousand four hundred and thirty-nine citizens declare on their federal income-tax returns that they earn at least a portion of their income by writing about fly fishing . . . or at least would like to do so." I told him that I got thousands of letters every year advising me that there were *fifty* million all-kinds-of fisher-men and every one of them would crave the proposed book. I told him that the best-selling fly-fishing book I'd published, thirty years ago, by some nifty students of the river, had sold a fraction of that number, and that the few books I'd written had sold a minuscule fraction of that fraction.

"But you don't know how explosive my concept is," Clyde said. "It will change fly fishing completely."

I sort of liked it the way it was but I merely muttered, "If I had a quarter for every time I've heard . . ."

"Don't be cynical. My concept involves the architectonics of flies, the astrophysics of fly casting, the morphology of rivers; it blends in tides, retrieves, wading, advanced leader construc-tion, rod repair, midstream lunches—all synthesized, brought into their cohesive and organic whole."

It sounded more like a drunken cook's smorgasbord, but I did not want to be mean to my old friend. In all the years I've edited books I'd seen a few of them march out into the world and conquer it, selling steadily and being genuinely helpful to a lot of fly fishers. And I'd seen a whole lot more descend into the darkness of oblivion on extended wings. I guess I'd survived as a publisher by being right a bit more than I was wrong, was all. I wasn't cynical, but I'd found that a bit of skepticism was the only way I could deal with the unending onslaught of proposals.

Over the years I'd had a number of proposals, such as Clyde's, that I simply could not afford, whatever their prospects. Only a few weeks earlier, I told him, a fellow had written me in broken English from Europe saying that he was pursuing a color theory—why fish were attracted to certain colors, and how they acted when they saw them—that was sure to revolutionize fishing. He said he needed only $25,000 a year for five or six years and he was sure to have the truly revolutionary results. Could I throw in a Pentium computer and life insurance for his family? I was sure to get back my bait with great interest since there were a hundred million fishermen in the world and I could have world rights . . .

Clyde said that color was not the key to fishing success. "Until we have the same optic structure and brain that fish do," he said, "we'll never know what they see. You were right to reject that proposal. But mine—"

"We've been friends for a great while," I said, remembering our childhood trips, the intensity with which we explored and fished then, the way Clyde ate worm sandwiches during one trip. "But I really don't think—"

"It's not a travel or mood book," he said, "like the one you once told me about—that fellow who wanted to fish all the way across the country . . ."

I remembered that proposal well. He was going to start in Virginia, with the first faint touch of spring, work his way up to the Poconos for the Quill Gordon, and then fish the Catskills, when the Hendricksons and March Browns were on. He'd fish the Hendricksons again, further north, then head for Michigan, following the major hatches so as to catch most of them; by early summer he'd be in Montana, where he could fish Pale Morning Duns, Brown Drakes, hoppers, Tricos, and then he'd push further west, to California, where he'd fish some of the spring creeks in the fall. He'd need a camper, of course, but could rent rather than buy that, and he wanted me to research the best local guides for him. "You can have the pleasure of lining up my itinerary," he told me. The trip could cost $23,786—he'd been very careful to keep costs down—and he'd want $50,000 for the writing, half on signing. He'd noted that one of the larger houses had paid $4.4 million for a *Gone with the Wind* spin-off a few months earlier. He was asking for a mere pittance.

"Me, too," I'd told him. "If you can find someone to fund such a trip, I'll go, too, and carry your rods."

I explained to Clyde my version of the economics of book publishing, and fly-fishing-book publishing in particular. I explained them at great length, using a pad to stress how difficult it was to make any money at it, how few people had been able to depend upon it for a living.

"So you think two hundred thousand is too much? Is that what you're telling me?"

"Yes," I said. "It's too much."

"How much isn't too much?" he asked. I mentioned a figure that made him snort.

"I couldn't pay my expenses for a week with that," he said.

I told him I understood, and that the book—to be done properly—would probably take him two years.

We were in my office and the phone rang. I told Clyde I'd have to take it—I was expecting a call from Kashmir, on a mahseer project—and turned from him. The call wasn't the one I was waiting for, but it was a proposal, and I repeated it, for Clyde's benefit. "Check out the rest of the Pacific for another Christmas Island?" I said. "Hire a seaplane? For three months? Four? Crew of three? Photographer?" Clyde was all ears. "Equipment? Of course. Yes. Clothing. Laptop computer?"

"Is he kidding?" whispered Clyde loudly.

I shook my head. No, this was serious. I was told about the magazine possibilities, the sale of information to travel agencies, outfitters, resort builders. I kept nodding. "Only two hundred and fifty thousand dollars? No. No, the figure doesn't scare me. Yes, a quarter of a million isn't a lot for such a pathbreaking voyage. I know. Yes. Well, no, I just don't think it's for us. Not today."

Clyde began to collect up his papers and shove them into the carryall he had brought. He kept shaking his head.

"Sounds like an interesting trip, actually. I guess I'd like to go on that one, too."

"Me, too," said Clyde. "But let's settle for a few bluegill in Ellis Pond, like the old days. I'd love that."

"Me, too."

14

HEAD WATERS

It is summer and when I turn on the faucet, despite the great drought upstate, water flows easily for as long as I like, ending its stop-and-start trip from wildness to what we call civilization. I watch for a moment, stunned by this rush of clear liquid I've seen ten thousand times before, then twist the faucet until the flow diminishes, trickles, and stops. The water may have begun on some remote hillside more than a hundred miles from my kitchen, but it has come more immediately from a city reservoir not a mile from my crowded apartment, or from one no more than a couple of dozen miles upcountry.

I once fished in such a nearby body of water, unceremoniously called "Reservoir 3," chiefly because my high-school friend Bernie, in Brooklyn, had it on good authority that the Canadian exhibit at the old Madison Square Garden Sportsmen's Show dumped their Atlantic salmon and ouananiche there. Bernie, our savant of stockings, was never wrong. And we were all mad to catch ouananiche.

We had seen them at the show one February, when, in the midst of a frozen winter, we longed for spring and the rivers that were our salvation; the fish were long, brilliantly spotted, with a bright reddish hue. There was something magical, exotic, about their name. We had caught only silvery trout, fresh from a hatchery, and these creatures from the wilderness of Canada absolutely exuded wildness. Besides, the name sounded Indian and we all wished we had that blood, or imagined we did. We tried desperately, fruitlessly, with worms, live minnows, spinning lures, and finally flies to extract even one from Reservoir 3—and in the end we had to settle for messes of crappie.

If you follow the liquid trail beyond such reservoirs—usually north, often joined by canals, pipeways, sluices, or man-made rivers to other reservoirs—you will find that in each, successively, the water is colder, the fish more beautiful. Crappie, bluegill, and perch give way to pickerel, largemouth, then smallmouth bass, which in turn, at higher elevations, become brown and rainbow trout.

The reservoirs, man-made, can provide fine sport, and so can the various waterways between them. In one such river, fed by one reservoir and running only three miles into another, I did most of my early trout fishing. It did not feel particularly artificial to me. I was a city kid and almost all flowing water was manna then. Even now, after I have fished the great chalkstreams of England and the greater spring creeks of the West, I go back to this river—and I still find in it a chance to practice certain hard-won truths, to fish over fish that have winced at scores of flies and in water that remains as familiar to me as my living room. The trout then, mostly stocked a few weeks earlier—Bernie knew to the dozen how many had been put in—brought us excitement, especially when we took a larger brown, one held over from the previous season. But we caught no ouananiche.

Above the last reservoir something else happens: the water is colder, clearer, mysterious. In one headwaters creek I know, high in the Catskill Mountains, the gradient steep and the riffles thin, everything is untouched by civilization—or, rather, con-

tinues to retreat from what is civilized. There was logging there
a hundred years ago. Telephone wires connect a remote wild-
life manager's cabin to the nearest town. Now and again some
kids walk in, leaving their bikes three miles below. The forest
is thick here, and the deadfalls tangle beneath your feet; there's
no way to make a living up that way. The river there is quick
and cold, even in summer. It's wilderness all right—good as
you'll find this side of Labrador.

In spring spate, the river rises ten feet and takes everything
in its path; I can see its marks well into the woods. In high
summer, like now, its flow oozes between exposed boulders
and is clear as water from a tap. The place is overhung with
hemlock, willow, and birch, so that the alley of the river is
intimate, shady. I have walked up there, skipping from stone
to stone when the summer heat is up, in sneakers, feeling the
cool water up to my calves, looking for pockets large enough
to hold a trout or two, perhaps with cold seepage from a spring.

There are such pools and runs and undercut banks, and a
dry fly pitched into them will bring a quick, eager spurt of
water. These trout are not selective feeders; they are through-
going opportunists and will take a Christmas tree of a Royal
Coachman as quickly as they'll rise to a fallen ant or bug. Once
I saw several large yellow stoneflies, *Perlas,* fluttering over one
of the larger pools, switched to a No. 6 Stimulator, and caught
a ten-incher, a prize in these small waters.

These are wild brook trout—five, six, sometimes eight
inches, on rare occasions a foot long. They have flanks as
smooth as an otter's skin, a dark mottled back, rose marks the
color of wild strawberries, and striped fins. They wiggle like
live jewels when you hoist them out of the water.

Greedy and wanton to their near extinction, vulnerable, full
of an innocence and hunger that cannot protect itself, these
fish are the ultimate emblems of piscatorial wildness, and it
delights me to catch a dozen on barbless hooks and slip them
swiftly back into their element. When I first climbed to the

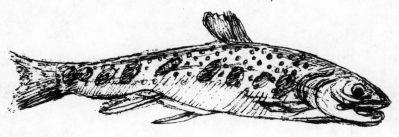

fountainhead of all city water and saw them, I stopped thinking of exotic Canadian fish and knew I had found a quiet place
that satisfied my subtlest longings for that which was *not*
civilized.

Little do those diminutive flashes of light and color know
the fate, downriver, of the precious, pure liquid in which they
flourish so unconsciously. Little do they care—so long as it is
there, so long as the great cities do not drink them to extinction. They are beautiful rare creatures and they dance in my
head, sustaining me, and I think of them even now, in the belly
of a great gray city, during the dog days of summer, every time
I turn on and turn off a faucet.

15

CONNECTIONS

Afriend, a naturalist who has not fished since he was a teenager and won't, on "moral grounds," asked me recently if I *had* to fish to be close to nature. Wasn't it cruel? Wasn't it unnecessary? I said hastily that this was one reason why I went to rivers. "But there's so much to see and touch and understand," he argued. "Must you pursue fish, too?"

Though I have fished since before memory and have never needed a "reason," his questions itched me, and the more I thought about them the more I realized I don't really go to rivers to "connect" with the natural world; I go to catch fish. I go with tackle that I have assembled over a course of many years: a rod I bought only last year because of its Space Age power and lightness; an old reel I'd found at a country red-tag sale thirteen years ago that worked like a fine watch; some flies I'd tied, but many dozens more that I'd selected with great care, after years of studying the design and architecture of these constructs, trying to imagine what a trout would see, what would best gull it.

I go with old patched waders and a vest crammed with fly dope, tweezers, a thermometer, two nail clippers, extra leaders, tippets, magnifying glasses for my old eyes, my wide-brimmed hat to keep sun off my forehead pocked with scars from basal-cell carcinoma surgeries, and much else. I take leaders I built myself, with materials I finally settled upon after years of trial, with the best knots I could learn. I wear exactly the socks that do not rub my shin-bone skin and a brand of sunglasses I winnowed from ten choices. I go with skills of sight and casting I honed over more than fifty years of going to rivers, and I feel very connected to all of my gear and to the balance of it all—its fitness for the job.

And I have learned how to use it all. I now choose my flies not only to imitate insects I might find, but for the attitude of those flies on the water, especially what I think the trout would see. Over the years I have learned how to approach trout and position myself to best advantage. I learned on certain water to use a 4-weight line rather than a 5-weight, so it would touch the surface less invasively. If I knew the trout in a river I'd be fishing saw too many ospreys and pelicans, I'd plan to make one false cast far to the right, over land, and then shoot the line once toward the fish I had located, trying not to cover it with line or leader.

I go to the river to catch trout. Everything I do depends upon that one fact. I am happy to think I am better skilled now than when I began, so many years ago. There may be sunsets, wildflowers galore, rainbows in the sky, good fellowship, good fishing, or lousy fishing; but what has drawn me here, the fulcrum of the entire equation, what will always draw me to water, is the simple prospect of catching a fish.

With luck—and some earned skill—the fly drifts a foot, two feet, and intersects with the fish's feeding lane. The fish that made the circle revealed itself to me individually, announced its intention to take lunch, is there, somewhere beneath the opaque, moving surface. I wait another second or two, then raise the fly smoothly into the air and cast again. This time, when the fly approaches the spot on the flowing surface where the trout rose, I feel the exquisite pleasure one feels when caught in any moment of suspense, of mystery: What will happen? There will be no "meaning" involved, only rejection or acceptance. The hesitation is palpable in the extreme and only later am I aware of how terrifyingly, blessedly concentrated I have been. The fly comes down to where the trout rose; the water pocks and bulges; I raise my rod slightly, and the fish and I are connected.

I need no more.

16

THE AGING FLY FISHER

As imperceptively as the growth of reason in a two-year-old, age comes to us all, even fly fishers.

At the latter end of the process you see it first in friends a dozen or more years older—how they don't move with the same speed they once did, when you suit up together, how they fuss with fly and leader a bit longer than you remember, as if cobwebs are covering their eyes or brain. You see it when their casts, for so many years smooth and accurate, drift inexplicably away from that rising trout you both stalked. You see it when they wilt before the day is three-quarters gone, as if a tank of gas were coming up empty, sputtering. You see it in the squint, the limp, the heavier breathing. You see it and call it "a bad week," "the extra thirteen pounds he put on this past winter," "a cold," "an ankle, mysteriously sprained." You don't believe it to be what it is—not for a minute—but you can't miss a telltale hint of the whole process.

I don't remember Charlie Brooks slowing down. I fished with him in his last years and he was always as vigorous and ani-

mated, in voice and movement, as ever. After a tough childhood during the Great Depression, years in the war, his body
began to break up when he passed middle age—gall bladder,
heart, this organ and that, bruised, failing. He'd always tell me,
after a tough bout, that he never felt better; he told me he fig-
ured that if they took an organ a year from him he had enough
parts left to carry him down the road quite far enough for his
purposes. And then suddenly, in his early sixties, he died.

Everything has its cycle, I guess—a school year that begins in
September and ends in late May or June, year after year, so that
the student lives by its rhythm. And even after it had ended—
after what seems an interminable number of years—it began
again for me, when I taught in a college, for twenty-six years.
The calendar year has its rhythm, too, beginning in the dead of
winter and progressing to late fall, when all is sere, and then
to the dead of winter again, when the world hibernates in cold
and snow. The fishing season is more logical: April, with its
great rebirth of earth and hopes, on through what my friend
Palmer Baker happily calls "the sweet of the year," into the dog
days of summer, and then the fleeting pleasures and surprises
and melancholy of fall. The fishing season is the one my blood
is chiefly keyed to—and I wouldn't have it otherwise.

All of these patterns are contained within the larger cycle
of a life—for fishermen, a fishing life. We start, somehow, many
of us, with some ineluctable tropism or tug toward water, toward a link with that bobber on a placid pond, the most electric object in our lives, its least movement telegraphed to our
heart. At not many years younger than I was when I fished such
a pond, my granddaughter has taken to asking, with great
regularity, about everything from a noodle to a bus, "Wha zat?"
It seems to be the emblem of something—the beginning of
knowledge, perhaps. Surely it was that when I began to ask,
as I watched the bobber and learned to decipher its faintest
movement, when I looked to the ring on the water or the little

splash made by a bluegill or small bass, when I saw the shadowy turn of something alive—eel, catfish, or perch—in the water's depths. "Wha zat?"—it led me to travel farther and farther afield, as I gained more independence and mobility; it led me to find new ways to fish, to understand more and more about my quarry, to "read" more and more into the great mystery that exists in that other world, beneath the surface. Perhaps the question led—it surely did for me—to fly fishing, for nothing could have seemed a more logical progression, based on hungers for more understanding as well as more challenges. In fly fishing I found all I wanted in fishing. And then other rhythms began, keyed to trout chiefly and to the foods they eat—from the first fumbling days with the clumsy long rod in my hands to halcyon days when I caught some of the largest and most difficult spring-creek trout imaginable. How many minuscule but telling questions led from the one day to the latest? And what fun I had at every turn.

For it is a happy progression, a seasoning of our timber, from bumbling to skill, from not knowing to knowing . . . but never all. Since fly fishing is—as Izaak Walton says—so much like the "Mathematicks" that it can never fully be learned, one's interest rarely falters, and mine hasn't. Nor does it with dozens of companions. I was with Len Wright the first time he went fly fishing for shad. I heard him say, as I heard him say on half a dozen new pieces of water, "What's the drill?" Then I watched him learn it by great concentration, and then, when he'd learned what someone else, more experienced, knew, he began to innovate. And he said it to me a dozen times, "Here's the drill," and I began to learn. That's part of aging, isn't it? Learning how to learn, assimilate, modify. It's not a bad route—and in fishing it doesn't seem to end.

Yes, it is easier to see aging in a friend than in oneself. From the slow changes to the abrupt, traumatic moments that punctuate our lives so dramatically and register their terrible changes, we see degenerating bone and muscle, the eyes that see less, the tightened residue of a stroke; they are not us and we read them better. Neither eye nor understanding really perceives what is happening to us until, mostly, it is reflected in someone else's comment or gesture, someone who helps us into a MacKenzie boat that we once could leap into, someone who offers to tie on a fly. Next, I thought, a few years ago, the man will want to help me pee.

Then, first, looking for it, I felt a certain dulling of what I heard, so that I didn't catch a friend's voice above the wind or a fly box slipping out of my pocket; and as I lost some hearing, I began to realize just how much it meant not to hear the whir of a swallow, the slurping rise of a trout; and I kept dropping clippers, knives, fly dope, and boxes, strewing fields with my smaller gear, not knowing I'd done so, losing it all forever. There came a time when I depended more and more upon my eyes— eyes that had read so much and learned to see the wink of a trout's mouth opening underwater—and then they began to fade, to see the world grayer, duller. When a gall bladder attack almost zapped me, and my limp proved to be an advanced dose of degenerative hip disease, I agreed with the maxim that growing old wasn't for sissies. There were reasons for all the tripping, for some of the new clumsiness I thought I'd lost forever. It's not that I don't like the genial optimism of Browning's "Grow old along with me/The best is yet to be," it's just that the hard facts mostly say otherwise.

But there are other changes—other choices—that come with age. We avoid water we know from forty years' hard experience to be dead. We choose the proper fly with less hesitation. We recognize the rise forms instinctively—instinctive after those forty years of looking—and false cast ten times less than we once did, because we now know how to pitch a fly with a lot less of the old fuss and because a fly line in the air cannot possibly advance our cause with Mr. Brown Trout. We may wade less treacherous water but we read all water better.

We may cast a shorter line but we know that coming much closer to a fish will give us a better chance. Because we know a few more of our limitations, and have those limitations, that doesn't mean for a moment that we can't look forward to even better—surely wiser—fishing in the years ahead.

Poised between what we can't and can do, still passionate about our fly fishing, though perhaps satisfied with a bit less, I find myself still asking the great question of my youth, with equal vigor and with ever new and undreamed answers: "Wha zat?"

17

FISHING, YEA, YEA

A *Wall Street Journal* article, filed from Ennis, Montana, reported that anti-fishing zealots had pelted with rocks the spot a fly fisher was fishing, then plastered his truck with their messages of nay. They want all fishing stopped—for bluegill, walleye, pike, carp, catfish, trout, the gentle bluefish, and Brother Crab—and the eating of them, too, of course.

There is now apparently a Crustacean Liberation Front to protect lobsters; and Mary Tyler Moore, the article reported, once offered $1,000 if a restauranteur would release a seventy-year-old, twelve–pound lobster (Rush Limbaugh offered $2,000 to eat it). That the fly fisherman eats less, if anything, of what he catches these days, means little here. We're talking about a charge of raw cruelty—and a fish struggling against the dangerous line or a hook in the lip is closer to the issue than the death we all owe, even lobsters.

Before I could smile twice and say, "Give me a break," I thought of several good friends who had abandoned their rods precisely because they no longer like the sight of that "live creature thrashing for its life." And I remembered a half dozen deer hunters I know who have stopped their sport (perhaps because the deer is closer to human size) and even a handful of bird shooters who have quit (in their case the most prevalent argument I've heard is that there are just too few grouse and woodcock left in their part of the world, their cover now malls or housing developments).

Fly fishers who throw fish back may seem more moral in this, but they merely have the opportunity to be more practical than hunters. It's more morally defensible, if defenses are necessary, to fish for food than to fish for pleasure, I suppose, though innocent pleasure has never been much of a sin to my way of thinking; and some friends who kill only stocked fish claim—and they're probably right—that they are improving the gene pool. The best reason to return fish remains Lee Wulff's pragmatic assertion, increasingly true, that gamefish are too valuable to be caught once—which, if I were a moralist, would imply an even less defensible moral position: doing the bad thing with the fish over and over again.

But I'm not a moralist, just an aging fisherman who has caught all manner of fish in a number of different parts of the world for sixty years and has never once questioned either his "right" to do so or the morality of fishing, and never will. I pursue fish because I like the mysterious challenge of gulling them to my fly, because I am enlivened by the intimate connection I then have to a wild creature, because I then like to bring them quickly to hand. I do so for my pleasure and recreation—which is a happy part of a full life—not for the fish's, and I am most concerned about their numbers and health not out of sentiment but mostly so that I can catch more fish, if I choose, and fish that are in better condition.

There, I've revealed myself as a hedonist of the first water: I pursue fish for my own selfish purposes and don't particularly fish for food, though I occasionally like to eat fish—and eating what you catch is a lost pleasure.

I am positive that my pleasure is no pleasure for Mr. Brown Trout. It may not feel with the same nervous system that we feel with; its mouth is not rimmed by the fleshy, sensitive lips we have; and it's cold-blooded, and only some human beings are such. But once hooked, a fish is definitely not comfortable. It would prefer to be near the bottom grubbing for crisp nymphs, rather than struggling against the restraining line, or still rising to those golden bon-bons floating above it.

The trout is not a human being and the repeated Disney-like, anthropomorphic assertions that a fish feels pain the way human beings feel pain are worse than simply misleading and spurious. They're downright dangerous. The anti-fishing and anti-hunting folk want fishermen to think in terms of human pain; but when Lord Byron in that infamous passage in *Don Juan* says that the "quaint, old, cruel coxcomb" Izaak Walton ought to have a hook in his gullet "and a small trout to pull it," he's sentimentalizing a fish's discomfort and severely undervaluing human pain, which civilization—with too many notable

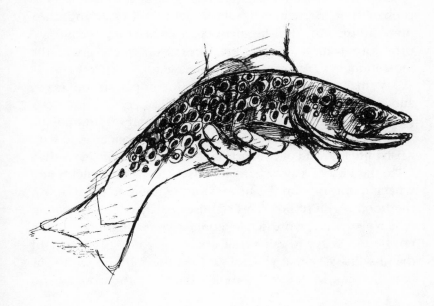

exceptions in our century—has generally tried to avoid since it stopped drawing and quartering, flaying, using the rack.

Consider the implications of this response Ed Zern received after a duck-hunting article of his appeared in *Audubon* magazine: "I hope you are shot in the gut," the nice bird-loving lady wrote, "and lie in a cold wet ditch and die slowly."

I don't enjoy watching any creature suffer—a mess of fish flopping on the bank or fish on a stringer, undulating listlessly, are unnecessary; I don't like to kill grasshoppers or any other wild creature slowly—except deer flies. I am the mortal enemy of Brother Deer Fly and kill every one I can, with impunity. After three of them have stabbed the tops of my hands, I grow to love the sweet crackling sound when I crunch them slowly.

Nature itself can seem pretty cruel. The heron will peck the back of a fish it cannot possibly lift from the water, leaving it disfigured, even disabled, for life. Lions begin to eat their prey while it is still alive. The gored lion dies slowly, abandoned by its pride, ravaged in the end by its mortal enemy, hyenas. A bluefish feeding frenzy is nature red in tooth and claw, but it is probably not, in the animal realm, cruelty at all, again an anthropomorphism. And fly fishermen, except when they become too profligate, wanton, in their pleasures, seem to me among the most innocent creatures in the universe.

My small contribution to the question of pain is the theory and practice of using the heaviest line, leader, rod, and hook possible. Ninety percent of my pleasure comes from hooking a fish. I don't find it more "sporting" to pussyfoot around with a fish until it's dead of exhaustion (or boredom), any more than I like the idea of a slow hangman. Get the fish in quickly and whack it abruptly on the head if you're going to eat it, or off the hook if you're not. This requires balance and judgment, which everything worthwhile requires: your equipment should not be too heavy to raise your quarry or your leader so light that it will assure that you will festoon the fish's lip with your Pale Morning Dun, size 18, thorax tie. Since the trout has no hands to help it extract flies, its having "won" the contest by breaking the too-light leader leaves it in worse shape than had it been caught by someone with both hand and hemostat.

Though we will never convince a skeptic that there is relatively little pain for the fish in the fish's scheme of things, we aren't the worse for thinking about the issue now and then. I suspect that part of my addiction to fly fishing, after a childhood spent with worm and spinner, has to do with the fact that bait often gets taken into the belly, with the hook, and a fish cannot be disengaged without harm. My old friend Louis Rubin has argued, wittily, that bait fishing is *more* moral because if a fish gets away at least it comes from the encounter with the tail of a worm, a bit of clam, for its efforts. But I guess that falls into the category of "fairness" to the fish rather than concern for its possible pain. Fairness? We use Space Age rods, watchlike reels, imported leaders, an arsenal worthy of General Schwarzkopf, for a creature with no brain as we know it at all.

The poet John Gay, disdaining nets, spears, trolling, and bait of all kinds, says, "Let me, less cruel, cast the feathered hook." I fish with a fly because it's more demanding for me, more intriguing in every way, and because it can be less cruel.

The world is full of a zillion sources of pain, from child molestation to genocidal wars to the medical problems of the folk next door, and one's own. And the tending of one's own house, the minding of one's own business, lost arts, are worth the worry far more than Disney anthropomorphism and, perhaps next, worry that cut plants may scream or rocks may cry. Don't those guys have anything better to do with their lives than save the carp and the lobster?

I love to think of generations of kids catching bluegill, as I did, with willow branches, stout cord, bobber, and worm, and those kids growing up to fish a fly to some pretty little brook trout or hundred-pound tarpon—and oh, cruel thought, would it cause great pain and suffering *to me* and a couple of million other folk to give up fishing forever.

Part Three

Some Books, a Mountain, and
My Painter Wife

MY FISH-BOOK LIFE

1 BERGMAN IN BROOKLYN

In my early teens in Brooklyn, I felt as far from the outdoors as from Outer Mongolia. Everywhere you looked there were dirt fields and cement—and our sports were city games: baseball on a field so stony that a mere grounder became a dangerous missile; stickball in the street, with the manhole in front of Ira's house as home plate; bike rides to Bensonhurst and Bushwick; stoopball; tough touch football in the fenced-in cement playground near P.S. 193; and a fierce brand of half-court basketball at Wingate Field that left most of us with torn and scarred kneecaps, elbows, and foreheads for life. There was no water closer than Steeplechase Pier at Coney Island—and the fishing there could only be rated as poor.

I had started to fish at my grandfather's hotel, the Laurel House, in an obscure corner of the Catskills, before memory. Then, fatherless, I continued to fish in a sump called Ice Pond during the grim years from four to eight at a frightening boarding school at Peekskill, where my growing passion for fishing

surely buoyed my spirits and possibly saved my life. When I was ten, my mother and my stepfather brought me to Brooklyn and the first thing I noticed was all the cement. The place was lousy with gray.

Summer camp, on Lake Ellis, in the foothills of the Berkshires, helped. I caught bullheads and bluegills there, on worms and doughballs, several varieties of other panfish, perch, and my first bass. On a picnic to Bull's Bridge on the Housatonic, I saw a magnificent trout rise to an unseen insect. The image never left me: the fish, nearly two feet long, starting as a shadow, turning into the shape of a trout, slipping downstream with the current, then angling up so gently that its white mouth barely winked, causing only a slight bending down of the surface and then a neat spreading circle, sliding downstream.

On cold November or December days in my teens I went to Steeplechase Pier with Mort and Bernie and used a two-ounce sinker, frozen spearing, and a thick glass rod to catch skate, hacklehead, and whiting and, in the spring, fluke, mackerel, and flounder. They were not pretty fish, and the fun of it was all contained in that little tug forty-five feet below and then the sight of a wriggling thing as we yanked a fish upward, reeling like mad.

Every afternoon during my early teens I worked for a gardener who tended lawns and backyards in the neighborhood. He was a high-school math teacher and I usually got to his house first, readied the tools, and then sat atop the bags of mulch and pungent fertilizer in the carryall he attached to his car, waiting for him to arrive. The job ended when I persuaded my parents to use his services and he had me do all that work for a buck an hour while he charged them four. But until the job collapsed, I used all the money I earned to buy my first spinning reel (a Mitchell), various lines, hooks, and lures, my first fly rod (made of white glass), and bait for many saltwater sojourns. I also subscribed to *Field & Stream, Outdoor Life, Sports Afield,* and *Fur Fish and Game,* which became my windows to the great world of angling beyond my gray universe. No one in my house

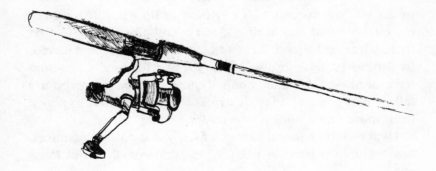

fished and my stepfather thought it pretty stupid, but each
month, when the magazines arrived, I fished in exotic places
with A. J. McClane and Joe Brooks, jumped off a bridge over
the Battenkill with Lee Wulff to see if you'd die in waders, fell
in love with Ted Trueblood's West, and got just a little better
at tackle-tinkering by reading "Tap" Tapply. Ed Zern taught me
to troll Johnson Silver Minnows from the back of a Fifth Avenue
double-decker bus.

Since I wouldn't become a collector for more than forty
years, I cut up these magazines, clipping the brightest, most
exotic color photographs with the biggest fish taken in extra-
ordinarily beautiful surroundings. In our unfinished basement
there was a coal bin, abandoned when we switched to oil; my
stepfather had built walls and a door to enclose the area, thinking to make a storage room of it, but like much else that he
started—marriages, relationships with his children—he abandoned the project. I swept and mopped it carefully, papered
every inch of the walls with the tear-outs from the magazines,
and tinkered with my tackle in that room for several years.

I read my first fishing books in that tiny room. I began with
Ray Bergman's *Trout,* as did most fishermen I know. I was looking for some logic to it all—the never-ending stream of tackle
and conflicting techniques, some understanding of the world
of rivers, which I had begun to fish—and Bergman's patient,
steady, thoughtful voice made sense out of the mysterious
world of trout fishing and the greater mysteries of why trout,
under various circumstances, behave as they do. He gave me
eyes to see what was in rivers, and even before I tied my first
fly to a leader, he gave form and focus to my eventual love of
fly fishing. He led me, also—as so many other angling authors
have done—to think as much about the respect I owed my
fellow fishermen and my quarry as I did about how to play a
trout more deftly once it was hooked.

I was mad then for news about fishing and learned advanced
bass techniques from Jason Lucas, an ethic from Roderick Haig-

Brown, something about the heart and soul of fishermen from Howard Walden's *Upstream and Down* and *Big Stony,* and with Ed Zern began to recognize that fishermen are in fact born honest . . . but they get over it.

These men were as much my heroes as DiMaggio and Duke Snider and Pee Wee Reese; they were as real to me as Ira and Billy and Jim, who lived on my block, whom I saw every day. Later, when I met most of them or corresponded with them, I felt that I was talking to old friends, that I had known them all of my life. Each was different; each affected me in his own way; each urged me closer to the heart or essence of a fly fisher's life—a life concerned always with immense respect for the rivers, without which there would be no fishing; with attention to the tackle and techniques and practical lore, without which one cannot become a player; with the words of their books, which record the history of fly fishing and chart its technical development and give us a binding philosophy and a common language; and of course with some less definable but no less potent quality—the "soul" of fly fishing.

In Brooklyn I knew no one who fly fished. My few fishing buddies and I, pariahs among the stickball and half-court basketball players, fished the pier at Sheepshead Bay and took wearying treks to trout country. We learned our language from the books and magazines; words were the hinge that drew us into something older and deeper and more various than we could possible have known.

Trout included a measure of everything one went to the word for. Of the three authors I read most intently, Bergman was surely the most practical. His early experiences, half a century earlier, paralleled mine—with their inescapable movement from "crude" to more refined, from unknowing to knowing. His instinctive dislike of hordes of people and of those "who are not in accord with the true spirit of nature," defined my own vague uneasiness with such people. Good art helps us see what we have passed a hundred times and have not seen, says Robert Browning in "Fra Lippo Lippi"; Bergman introduced me to wet flies, streamers, nymphs, and dries, and how they should be used; he described water types I'd seen and had begun to understand from my worming and spinning, and told me how to fish them with flies, which sometimes was not so different from the ways I'd learned; he studied the effects of sunshine and shadow, and he recorded experiences that helped me to understand how trout reacted to a dozen kinds of weather. And all this was before I tied my first fly onto a leader.

Haig-Brown taught me something else, begun in Bergman but always subverted there to the man's wonderfully practical bent. *A River Never Sleeps,* following the seasons of the year and the seasons of a fly-fishing life, drew me deeply into the kind of earthy, spiritual connection one can have with rivers and fly fishing. Haig-Brown, fishing a part of the world (British Columbia) I have not yet fished, often for a fish I've not yet caught (steelhead), spoke of the abiding love all fly fishers have for moving water, anywhere. I cannot think of a passage that better defines this than the resonant ending to that remarkable book:

> I still don't know why I fish or why other men fish, except that we like it and it makes us think and feel. But I do know that if it were not for the strong, quick life of rivers, for their sparkle in the sunshine, for the cold grayness of them under rain and the feel of them about my legs as I set my feet hard down on rocks or sand or gravel, I should fish less often. A river is never quite silent; it can never, of its very nature, be quite still; it is never quite the same from one day to the next. It has its own life and its own beauty, and the creatures it nourishes are alive and beautiful also. Perhaps fishing is, for me, only an excuse to be near rivers. If so, I'm glad I thought of it.

Howard Walden's books touched me to the bone. They were about Eastern, often Catskill, waters, which I was beginning to know well, and the voice of that gentle, wise, and sensitive man began to color my own. Nowhere, I think, is the revelation of catching a first trout (while one is fishing for coarser fish, in this case shiners) better rendered than in the chapter "The Spark Is Kindled." Here, finally, is a fish so exquisite that it puts all others to shame; here is a fish that calls forth finer, more thoughtful qualities from you than shiners, bluegill, or perch; here is a fish made for fly fishing, a fish that demands you fish with a fly.

In *Upstream and Down* Walden meditates on the various stripes of fishermen, on methods and fish sense and luck and gear; and he defines again, and finely, as so many fishing writers have tried to do, much of the "why" and the "how" of fly fishing. *Big Stony* is different. It is one of those rare works of fishing fiction—a small list that includes some stories by Robert Traver, Hemingway's "Big Two-Hearted River" and *The Old Man and the Sea,* and Norman Maclean's *A River Runs Through It.* And insofar as stories touch us in deeper ways than sermons, the tales of this fly-fishing club, "The March Brown Fly-Fishing Club," moved me then beyond anything I had yet read. To this day, more than forty-five years after I first read them, I remember the pathos of Lank Starbuck's death in "Old Poacher's Return," the human challenge and triumph in "Challenge at the Elbow," and the moving story of a boy becoming a man in "When All the World Is Young."

After I began to fly fish seriously, in my mid-twenties, these books lived in me and I went back to them time and time again. But my reading branched off and broadened: I read for knowledge and historical perspective and for the literature; having studied and taught the latter, I now made greater demands on what I encountered, insisting that it transcend the "Me and Joe" stories, the tearjerkers, the easy cliché-ridden sentimental tales that I read everywhere.

Out of the vast gray of the past I plucked such gems as Alfred Ronalds's *The Fly-Fisher's Entomology,* the books and speculations of F. M. Halford and G. E. M. Skues (whose story "Mr. Theodore Castwell," about a man whose fishing in Hell is *too* good, is one of the treasures of the sport), John Waller Hills's *A Summer on the Test,* and Lord Grey of Fallodon's *Fly Fishing.* These were from the British tradition but they were the foundation of our fly-fishing tradition, too; and America's tradition was growing. I soon found John McDonald's *The Complete Fly Fisherman: The Notes and Letters of Theodore Gordon,* and Preston Jennings's pathbreaking entomology *A Book of Trout Flies.*

Closer to our time, practical writing became more exactingly practical and we began to get some first-rate bug books. Ernest Schwiebert's essential *Matching the Hatch* came out in the mid-1950s and created a great flush of interest in imitation that had not existed when *Art Flick's Streamside Guide to Naturals and Their Imitations* (still one of the best basic introductions to the concept of imitation I know) and Vincent C. Marinaro's brilliant *A Modern Dry-Fly Code* (which created an ethic and logic for dry-fly imitation) appeared less than a decade earlier.

Mostly, though, I began to realize that some glue must hold all this knowledge together. In the best stories about fishing, by our best writers, we find the heart and soul of fly fishing. Odd, funny things happen; there is mystery and suspense, challenge and discovery; the words have the warm colors of earth and water, not the bland jargon of the specialist; we meet real people, who happen to be fly fishers; big fish are caught or lost; and when we have finished such stories or books we understand much more about our passion to fly fish.

Such is surely the case with Sparse Grey Hackle's story "Murder," about a man who catches a gigantic trout while trying to escape the doldrums of the Depression and discovers that even fishing won't let him flee the world of affairs; and with William Humphrey's hilarious dissection of days (and nights!) in a Scottish salmon-fishing hotel, *The Spawning Run;* and in dozens of shrewdly witty essays by Ed Zern; and with Norman Maclean's haunting memoir of fishing with his father and brother in Montana, *A River Runs Through It;* and with any of a half dozen stories and essays by the distinguished novelist Thomas McGuane, or poems and stories and essays and passages in novels by Seamus Heaney, Craig Nova, Jim Harrison, John Engels, David Quammen, W. D. Wetherell, Ted Leeson, or an increasing number of other superb contemporary writers and poets.

I still love the old, nostalgic fly-fishing classics, and all they did to fashion the way I think and feel about the sport; and I'm delighted that the best of the younger writers have found in fly fishing sufficient depth for some of their best writing. But what interests me most about today's best writing about fly fishing is that it is realer and sharper, less idealized, less part of the specialized tradition of fishing writing and closer to just plain good writing. If this is a sign that fly fishing is being thought of more as a part of life than apart from it, I'm delighted; for the best writing about fly fishing—from Walton to Bergman to McGuane—not only says a few things that make us shrewder fly fishers but also a few that make us wiser human beings.

2 WRITING AND TEACHING

As late as my early thirties I had neither the training nor the experience to write or edit. I had studied economics at the Wharton School of Finance and Commerce of the University of Pennsylvania, where I had spent my energies to earn a letter in basketball, and only my passion for fishing matched that of anyone, anywhere—not my skills or experience. Sometime during my Army years, when basketball and baseball became the games of my youth and I had presumably finished my formal schooling (though I felt dumb as a slug), I felt a growing restlessness about what I was going to do—and be—when I grew up.

I remember a scorching Kentucky afternoon at Fort Knox, where I was shipped after I finished basic training—when I took a notebook onto a quiet field and wrote for four hours. I don't remember what I wrote, though I know it wasn't about fishing. I suspect it was about one or another incident from my college years. I wrote until my fingers ached, feeling a growing excitement with words, with storytelling, and when I stopped, for the first time, I felt the pain of a bright red sunwelt between my pants bottom and the top of my sock. It was a severe, uncompromising pain—and the concentration that allowed it, a concentration of energy and vision that I'd never felt before, told me that when I grew up my life would be centered on words.

For six months after I left the Army I lived alone in a snot-green room on West Tenth Street in Greenwich Village. The room—once a walk-in closet or a john—was exactly four and a half strides long. The bed wedged sideways into two snug alcoves at the far end; there was a sink whose porcelain had been gnawed away in a dozen places by rust; there was a hot plate, a tiny desk, one chair. On one of the walls a previous tenant had hung a Christ with a crown of thorns, ripped from a magazine and put carelessly into a Woolworth frame. The half window over the bed opened into the alleyway of a posh restaurant, and on warm spring nights, I could hear the constant clanking and clinking of dishes, smell a dozen amiable mixed scents, and hear occasional high laughter. I wrote, often for a dozen hours or more a day, not for fame or glory—or even money—but to still some great hunger in my heart.

Still, every morning after I had lingered in the dark hallway for a glimpse of Diane, the young ballet dancer next door, I checked my mailbox. Since I wrote at a ferocious rate and sent my miserable words out into the world like so many arrows, randomly shot, the mailbox was host to a steady stream of rejections. At first, all of the rejections were printed notices to the effect that (a) the magazine received a huge number of submissions; (b) someone had in fact read what I had scraped off my brain; (c) what I had done was not—for some exceptionally good but unnamed reason—for them. *The New Yorker* returned my poems and stories so fast that, in the mad blur of those intense days in the mid-1950s, I often thought I had submitted the work the day before, or even that morning.

During those early years—perhaps five or six of them—I made time to write stories and poems and to submit them, and every last scrap of paper came back. I can remember having several shoe boxes filled with rejection notices—thousands of those antiseptic slips, mostly uncontaminated by human word. How I leaped when I finally received a first "try us again" or a "not bad" or a scrawled "not quite for us but thanks." An underlined "quite" or an exclamation point after the "thanks" was cause for great hope. A signed letter from another human being made me levitate.

Narcotics, writes Emily Dickinson, "cannot still the tooth / That nibbles at the soul." I had one helluva big tooth chewing on me in those first years I began to write, and those days in the tiny snot-green room were raw, frustrating, painful, even comical. There was too much to know. I was too dumb. So at twenty-six I went back to school as a freshman on the G.I. Bill, to Bard College, where I fell in love, married, then trailed my wife to the Cranbrook Academy of Art in Michigan, and went on, with ferocious longing, for an M.A. and then a Ph.D. in English from the University of Michigan. I taught briefly at Michigan, we had four children before you could say "enough," and I soon found myself in New York City with three full-time jobs.

Two of the jobs were teaching (at Hunter College) and proofreading (at Crown Publishers); the third, always, I considered writing. At first I wrote literary criticism—about Kafka, Thomas Nashe, Chrétien de Troyes, Tolstoy, Melville, minor poets like Jones Very—and published thirty or forty poems, all in literary magazines like *The Michigan Quarterly* and *The Yale Review*. But not until the mid-1960s, when I was in my mid-thirties, did I write my first fishing memoir. I called it "First

Trout, First Lie," and it was the simple story of how, at five or six, I caught my first trout from a Catskill creek by gigging it in late summer with a Carlisle hook strapped to a willow branch, and then promptly lied, out of pure snobbishness, that I had caught it in a more "moral" way, on a worm. I was by then even more advanced in my knowledge of rejection slips than I had been in the snot-green room; I had a galaxy of shoe boxes now, containing "No"s from almost every major magazine in the northern hemisphere. I had become convinced that *The New Yorker* had a special Reject Agent at the main New York City Post Office on West Thirty-third Street. But this story felt different. It had come not out of a desire to write anything, or an assignment, but out of some urgency to share a particular story that had lodged in my brain for nearly thirty years. I might not know about Argentina and dorado, but I had lain on the weathered boards of that old bridge, watched the dimpling sunfish, spotted the nose of the great trout protruding from under the base of the bridge, eased the long hook into its mouth, and yanked. I had done that. I knew that. And no one else did.

Writing this story, I found a different voice, free of academic cant, free of artistic pretension, free of preaching, free of what was fancy-dan or trendy. Writing about something I had loved for so long I found a voice—earthy, nimble, wry, full of wit and worms and celebration. I had always put on purple robes before I wrote critical prose, fiction, or poetry; but this story had in it the mud of the creek and the point of a Carlisle hook. I sent it at once to *Field & Stream* and a week later got a matter-of-fact thirteen-word letter from Clare Conley, saying, "We like your story and a check will go out to you shortly." I had no trouble memorizing it. He didn't sound very excited but I was: I showed the letter to everyone I knew—doormen, store managers, Uncle Al, the chair of the English Department, colleagues at Crown—and promptly sat down to write another, which also came easily, "Mecca," about Frank Mele, a great old friend I called Hawkes, and a memorable trip from Woodstock to the Beaverkill.

I sometimes wonder if I'll ever write stories as good as those first two, which were given to me, but I keep trying.

I showed both stories to my friend Emile Capouya, whose heart is larger than most, and he encouraged me to write a book's worth of them, "a mélange of poetry and technology." He did more than "encourage": he gave me a contract. I called the book *The Seasonable Angler* and it was still in print, thirty years later, the last time I looked.

Over the next thirty years I published some three hundred articles and stories, more than a dozen books; I did too much ghostwriting for a while, one book a best-seller, and also wrote this and that, here and there, mostly on fishing. One chair of the English Department at Hunter College said that I was an embarrassment to them, writing so many fishing stories, and would never be promoted; I should get on with my professional writing—"Twenty-seven Brands of Ambiguity in 'The Quarter-deck' Chapter of *Moby-Dick*" perhaps—but by then I was too badly gut-hooked by fish-tales. I did not like, or want to re-read, the critical articles I'd published in *The Michigan Quarterly* and a dozen other literary magazines; I had stopped writing such prose—and since then the closest I've come to them has been an occasional book review for *The New York Times, The Pennsylvania Gazette, The Baltimore Sun.* Four terms later, a new chair, who had fished for something somewhere and had enjoyed it, put my name up for Full Professor, and at the Faculty Personnel and Budget Committee hearing I was asked to speak about "The River as Metaphor in World Literature"—a balloon ball in the ninth inning if there ever was one. So I told them about Roderick Haig-Brown and Ted Trueblood and Joe Brooks and Norman Maclean (whom no one knew then, so I referred to him simply as the William Rainey Harper Professor of English at the University of Chicago), and quoted off the cuff from Al McClane's "Song of the Angler," as well as from Twain and Hesse, and as no one had heard of the first five, they thought I must therefore be very smart and well informed, and I sailed through with colors quite as bright as those of a Royal Coachman.

3 FINDING FLICK—AND OTHERS

My parallel life as a full-time editor began only two years after I began to teach, in 1964. I switched to the evening session at Hunter College and raced by subway every day from Crown Publishers to the college, where my classes began at 5:40; the trip took twelve to thirteen minutes most nights, sometimes forty. I began on a two-week trial basis, as a proofreader and checker of mechanicals. After that time I met the editor in chief in the bathroom and asked if I could stay. He simply nodded and smiled and I thus began a thirteen-year period of my life when I edited full-time, taught a full program of up to five courses, and took on four major book ghostwriting assignments—about the mother of a president, for a feminist, for a veterinarian, and for an adopted woman who had, after twenty years of searching, found her natural parents. And I began to do more and more writing of my own. They were whirlwind days, trying to be sensible with my four growing children, ambitious at Crown, wise at Hunter, selfless in my ghostwork. I can remember one period of five weeks in which I wrote a woman's autobiography, took eurythmy classes at six every morning, worked a full schedule as executive editor at Crown, and taught three summer classes. What energy I had then— and how I used every last bit of it, and more!

By 1968 I saw that I would have to start signing up books of my own if I wanted to stop reading proof, and I had no eye for commercial fiction or books about nudists or macramé or Asian politics. I had been looking for a copy of Art Flick's old *Streamside Guide to Naturals and Their Imitations,* which had been published in 1947 and soon abandoned, and couldn't find one; every tackle store I asked told me that it ought to be reprinted, that lots of fly fishermen wanted a copy. I'm not quick, but by the fifth time I got the idea. But the chiefs at Crown said they had once published a fishing book and that it flopped. I persisted and I think in the end Crown threw me a bone—or a bug—and that book became the first in my Sportsmen's Classics series, after a short debate about how it should be produced. I suggested that, as a streamside guide, it might fruitfully be done with a waterproof jacket and binding; the president of Crown, an old pirate, responded to the effect that we ought to give it a *lead* binding, so that if it fell into a river the fisherman would have to buy another.

I put together an anthology that year, *Fisherman's Bounty,* and from that I was suddenly in contact with a dozen fine writers about the sport, including Vince Marinaro, whose *A*

Modern Dry-Fly Code (at Mele's strong insistence) I soon re-published. I also republished Preston Jennings's *A Book of Trout Flies* and, at Art Flick's suggestion, *Selective Trout,* a new book by a couple of young whizzes he'd met recently. The books did well. Marinaro's, which had sold fewer than 700 copies when it was first published in 1950 by Putnam's, sold more than 15,000 copies; the Jennings, whose minimal sales had disappointed that great author sorely, sold out four print-ings; *Selective Trout* was an instant success and, over the past twenty-five years, has sold more than 175,000 copies. But my greatest pleasure was to persuade Sparse Grey Hackle to ex-pand *Fishless Days,* a book privately printed by The Anglers' Club of New York, into *Fishless Days, Angling Nights.* The editor in chief almost let that big one get away, too. I proposed it to him, Sparse agreed to the terms, and Crown then sat on the contract for six months. Sparse, with a backbone and pride like steel, balked and demanded his manuscript back. I returned it but kept cajoling him. He finally relented and I published the book with immense love for the great old fellow and for his prose. What fun we had—and what good friends we became! And the book did well enough for me to win a big bet from Sparse—about which more later.

Sparse and I talked often about words, and he chuckled and chided me for my softness when I told him that I thought Flick could do no wrong and allowed a reference to "love yarn" to go through galleys and into the finished book. I'd been too embarrassed to ask the "stupid question": What is it? For two years Art got letters asking where this miraculous stuff could be got and told each person to look instead for *olive* yarn. "Olive," Sparse and I agreed, was a jinxed word. He, who was meticulous with words, told me that he stopped writing for *Sports Illustrated* after they made an editorial change in an article of his. Referring to his friend L. Tappen Fairchild, a devout dry-fly fisherman, Sparse had written that this great pur-ist had once, to his shame, deigned to use an "olive nymph."

Sports Illustrated thought an olive nymph an absurdity so they changed it to "live" nymph—which must be the most libelous change of one letter ever made.

At first I worked alone at Crown—selecting, editing, even marketing the books. Crown was a freewheeling place then, with some warts but also with a great capacity to let an editor play out his hand in his own way. It seemed axiomatic to me that the single best place to sell fly-fishing books was in a tackle shop, few of which carried books then, so I began to clip ads, accumulate the addresses of stores across the country one by one, and file the names on three-by-five-inch index cards. Then I'd send each a flyer, a personal letter (I still use a manual typewriter and do all my own correspondence), and some follow-up material. I did this regularly, every day, even obsessively. It was not especially clever of me; but I was a bulldog about it and we soon had some one thousand new accounts in the field. You can publish the best fly-fishing books of all time, but if you don't find a way to sell them, the business will not survive. It's as simple as that.

Those were exciting years. I felt that we (Jerry Hoffnagle, fresh from Penn State, came aboard to help me in the early 1970s) were breaking new territory constantly and that getting more good fly-fishing books out and into the hands of fly fishers was a thing of true value. I can remember hand-carrying books to Abercrombie & Fitch and to Jim Deren's crowded Anglers' Roost in the Chrysler Building; arranging signings for Sparse at William Mills and at Trout Unlimited banquets; devising posters, writing (with Jerry) the *Sportsmen's Classics Newsletter,* which got mailed to everyone we could think of. We were unsystematic, tenacious, self-mocking (we once included some choice passages from authors we published, like Charles Ritz's odd maxim "Never fish downstream from a Belgian"), hugely enthusiastic, evangelical, and passionate about everything we did. People who were more intimately connected to their sport, we reasoned, through a vehicle like the broad literature of fly fishing, would do more to protect it—its ethics, its best practices, the conservation of the resources, without which it could not be protected. I still believe this to be so.

Then, in the mid-1970s, there was suddenly a glut of fly-fishing books, a nasty bit of cutthroat discounting, a flatness to the market, and, for me, a sharp rebuke from Hunter College, which demanded that I stop holding two full-time jobs, though my teaching (I argued) was only better for my knowledge of the practical world of publishing.

I had by this time published or republished in the Sportsmen's Classics series some fifty-two books, most on fly fishing, including such older and new titles as Roderick Haig-Brown's seasons series, his *Return to the River,* and *A River Never Sleeps;* Howard Walden's two fine books, in one volume; Marinaro's new *In the Ring of the Rise;* Robert Traver's warm *Trout Magic;* Lefty Kreh's pioneering *Fly Fishing in Salt Water;* my friend Mike Migel's *Stream Conservation Handbook;* a second book by Doug Swisher and Carl Richards; some important fly-tying books, like *Art Flick's Master Fly-Tying Guide* and Robert Boyle's and Dave Whitlock's *The Fly-Tyer's Almanac;* Eric Leiser's excellent *Fly-Tying Materials;* and a raft of others. I liked then, and still do, the concept of mixing reprinted older books of true importance and the best new books I could find. I especially liked reprinting those books that I'd first read in my basement in Brooklyn.

Then Jerry went to Stackpole and I, for a number of reasons, quit the publishing world, I thought forever. I'd had a good run, and I was writing more myself then, and I was still very much devoted to my teaching. This fish-book publishing had been a kind of secret life, after all.

Crown did not seem disappointed when I left. They had embarked on a fast track, with million-dollar advances to best-selling authors like Judith Krantz, and my fly-fishing books were mere minnows.

In 1978, Timothy Benn, a publisher and fly fisher from England, came to me and asked if I'd start an American subsidiary for him in the colonies, using my name as the corporate trading name; we'd publish books on fly fishing and other outdoor leisure sports. He wanted me to function as a packager—a producer of books that were immediately sold, in their entire edition, to another publisher, who then handled all sales, promotion, and distribution. He picked Doubleday as our partner, and within a few years, working out of my living room with the help of several freelancers, I'd produced eight books for them and engineered their purchase of John Goddard's and Brian Clarke's *The Trout and the Fly* and Jackie Wakeford's *Fly-Tying Techniques.* Both were produced by Timothy's English staff and both are excellent books and sold very well over here. My first book was William Humphrey's *My Moby Dick.*

The Doubleday relationship matured and then rotted, and I had an increasingly disembodied sense, as I produced the books and then lost all control of them to people for whom they might have been widgets or pickles. It was less and less fun.

But the Benn group would not budge on the issue of packaging—which fuels its own growth—and Doubleday clearly did not want either the more technical fly-fishing books (like Gary LaFontaine's *Caddisflies*) or as many books as I now wanted to publish; in fact, I had begun to publish more and more outside of the fly-fishing field—in other outdoor leisure sports, in natural history, in art, in adventure. I went to Winchester Press with the fishing books, to Schocken and W. W. Norton with those on other subjects. My fish-book life was growing more scattered, untidier and untidier.

I had an office now—or, rather, I sublet a room from another small publisher—and I hired Peter Burford (whom I had met when he was a senior at Princeton) to help. Three years later I made him a partner, and then recently he left to start his own firm.

Soon after Peter came to work for me, Benn Brothers was taken over by a company with the awful name of Extel; and we were told that the new U.K. owners had no interest in books, especially not in fly-fishing books, and that we would be sold off if we did not offer enough for the business ourselves. Since I was then the principal asset, I said I refused to be sold; and since I did not think I should have to pay much for myself, I bid what the Benn negotiator called "two peanuts." Six months later they agreed to the same offer, and I raised $100,000 from seven fly-fishing friends (enough to buy the business and keep us afloat for a few months), put up some cash, and had a nice little untidy business, whose books were scattered around the industry and whose sole occupation was still packaging books for others.

Though we did some good books during those early years of independence, the work was perpetually frustrating. At first we continued to package books—out of financial necessity. Our staff was minuscule and our second office was cramped—five hundred square feet, which we shared with a lunatic whose greatest joy was to buy a carload of impounded Maharini furniture and who once caused me to send the small staff home when he went fully off the wall and had a shotgun available to him. When we bought the business we moved to quarters three times as large as we needed—and nearly went bankrupt; we lost, for the first time in my publishing life, and with great pain, a whole slew of fine first authors; we contracted for books that no other publisher would buy from us; and I found increasingly that I no longer had the energy to edit and teach and write full-time. Something would have to change.

Within the last ten years I did those things necessary to provide the independence needed to publish as I think best—with maximum freedom. I took great risks to bring all the functions of a publishing house under one roof, to consolidate and focus everything I do.

I bought back all the books I'd packaged for Doubleday; I bought all stock and rights to the books I'd edited at Crown that were still viable; after some bitter disputes with Winchester, I made a bid for all the books we'd packaged for them and it was eventually accepted. I cannot think of another publishing firm that has bought back its packaged books like this—but I was convinced that the books had much more life in them, or that we could breathe life into them, and we have been proved right.

We hired an outside sales manager for several years, an experienced hand who plugged us into five groups of book sales reps; we set up a surrogate group of sales representatives for the sporting field; we installed a computer, hired a biller, began to build our own lists, and, gradually, learned how to market our own books. I changed the name of the business from Nick Lyons Books to Lyons & Burford, to reflect Peter's status. I retired from teaching after twenty-eight years to devote my best energies to publishing. And we began to increase the number of books we published in fields other than fly fishing, to reduce our dependency on that one field, however deeply loved.

Art Flick's little guide still sells a thousand copies a year; a new stream identification guide on our list, done (by the grace of the new technologies) in full color, has not supplanted it. Doug Swisher and Carl Richards did a new book with me recently, and we have published revisions of some of the old Sportsmen's Classics books from Crown, including *Fly Fishing in Salt Water* and *Practical Fishing Knots.* New authors, like Tom Rosenbauer, Dave Whitlock, and Dick Talleur, bring great practical experience to their books—and they have sold very well; some people I edited twenty years ago have moved on to larger and what they consider better houses, for much larger advances than we offer.

In recent years the market has changed and matured; many reviewers have—thankfully—become more demanding; more books celebrating the pictorial pleasures of fly fishing are being published; our "market share" has surely diminished, though we're publishing more fly-fishing books than ever; several aggressive wholesalers handle an increasing percentage of the book business we do with tackle shops; more publishers are "trying on" a fly-fishing book or two, to get in on a "hot" field; many authors have decided to self-publish; several "continuity" programs for books in the field have been very successful.

I don't think I'll ever again experience the excitement I felt when I signed up Art Flick's book and saw it prepare to take wing, or the day Sparse dropped by, placed his manuscript back on my desk, and said, "All right, Bub, you can publish it—but it won't sell a thousand copies" (he was, for once, dead wrong; we sold thirteen thousand); or that evening we arranged to get all of our sporting books back from Winchester Press and consolidated our independence.

I never wanted to be a latter-day Derrydale Press, and we're not at all like that distinguished sporting-book house; we're not as exclusive, not focused only on sport, and we do little that compares with Eugene V. Connett's brilliant bookmaking. But I'm proud of our list.

Peter Burford left the firm in 1997 and I changed the name of the business yet again, this time to The Lyons Press. My son Tony, a lawyer, has come aboard and is n   sident. We're perhaps a midsized rather than a small pul   g house now, but still fiercely independent, financially so   reasingly diverse, full (I think) of surprises, and alway   r to publish books better.

4 BUILDING A LIST

For many years, then, I have spent much of my life thinking about the words of angling—making some myself, reading those of others (some written hundreds of years ago), publishing a lot of others, even fixing some by people who are superb fishermen but not as good writers.

I now get some six to seven hundred book submissions a year, and the number continues to build. Some are from folks I've published before, but most are from the vast legion of fishermen for whom the sport seems uniquely able to prompt words. Sometimes it appears as if everyone and his mother-in-law wants to write a fishing book.

Some years ago I had finished fishing the Buffalo Ford section of the Yellowstone, had caught enough cutthroats and seen enough brothers and sisters of the angle to decide I'd never fish there again, and was wading briskly toward the parking lot. There were as many cars as you'd see in a suburban mall during a Saturday sale in October. Looking up, I saw someone point in my direction—and a moment later a tall man began to stride through the shallows toward me. I wondered why he had no rod in his hand. But he held before him—as if it were his most prized possession, or perhaps a summons he intended to serve on me—a manila envelope. I had seen its like before. I could not turn back without disrupting, for the second time, the sport of the couple dozen tightly bunched fisherfolk I'd just passed, so I stopped, waited for the man, and in a few moments— his face full of smiles—he neared me and said, "Boy, have I got a present for you!"

It was a manuscript, of course, and I suppose I was so shocked to be handed one from a perfect stranger in the middle of the Yellowstone River that I did not drop it into the drink at once; but I never think of the proper comeback until a full week after someone has said something sharp to me. Later, raw curiosity—which will kill me someday—proved quickly and conclusively that it was a very bad manuscript indeed, ill-conceived, poorly written, without structure or point.

That should have warned me to accept such paper only when I'm at my desk. But I'm a slow learner and failed to turn down a kind offer a fellow made to me the next spring at the Suffern Fishing Show to send on "a little" of his writing, which he just thought I'd "enjoy a lot"—the offer, made with an innocent smile that appeared to say "six pages' worth," metamorphosed into an orange crate full of random scribblings, diatribes, notebook after notebook about fishing that I "might like to make a nice little book from"—if I had the time and happened to be Maxwell Perkins, which I don't and I'm not.

Because of these episodes and dozens like them, I have grown oddly allergic to manuscripts that arrive while I am fishing or browsing or engaged in some other amiable activity, as I have always been allergic to unseparated printouts, especially when they print out faintly, to handwritten manuscripts, to rough-edged piles of tear sheets, to *any* fishing book over 417 pages, unless it's written by John McDonald.

I have had proposals from he who wants, with straight face, $250,000 of my little business's money to charter a small aircraft and explore every atoll in the South Pacific, looking for another Christmas Island bonefish bonanza. Me, too. Much more modest and pragmatic was a crisp but definitive treatise on catalpa worms, covering their propagation and use as bait, with the author's personal guarantee that he'd give me a lifetime supply of the succulent little darlings, an opportunity on which I passed. Most common are the scores of reminiscences—from people who only fish, all day, every day, to those who solve midlife crises and "find themselves," waist deep in a remote river. I suppose all of this river immersion is better than psychotherapy—and at least more fun to do, if not to read about—but I fear daily that fly fishing has made writers of us all. Even at my lower weight classes I never wanted to be a ballet dancer; few people do, though most of us do a bit of dancing. But everyone who fishes and can write his name wants to write a fishing book. The mere catching of a fish is somehow such a potent triumph that it deludes all of us into thinking we know enough to write a book. The happiness or drama of a day afield is so persuasive that each of us thinks his experience unique and meriting the permanence of print. No one has seen such a sunset, such a rise, such a cast. No one has had such scintillating streamside conversation, in italics. No one has a pal like Joe.

I must make decisions on each proposal, and my little firm will prosper or head south depending upon the wisdom with which I do. Decisions must mediate between what is worthwhile, what is new, what will sell. If the business vanishes, the other questions don't count—and small publishing ventures are the most vulnerable business entities I know. A friend whose small publishing firm failed twenty-odd years ago recently wrote in an autobiography that in the seven years he did business, he lost his substantial inheritance, the family salt farm in Rhode Island, a sizable portion of his uncle's fortune, most of his wife's money, his wife (who left him), his son (because she took him to France for the rest of his childhood), and "the use of my name for the rest of my life." The last phrase, if not the details that precede it, is chilling.

I reject for any of a thousand reasons: the work is poorly done, it is on a subject that does not interest me, it is too expensive to produce, it would take more time than I have to give it the proper shape according to my lights—or for even less tangible reasons: I don't know why but I just don't want to do it. It may be good or even great; it may be something someone else will publish gleefully, and I hope they do. I did not hang out a shingle and say, "I will surely give you good and proper reason if I don't decide to invest my time and money in your book."

Am I obliged to do so?

I don't think so. Quietly, as I try to keep a small publishing house afloat, I have to say that I do not—cannot—offer myself to the world as a free reader of manuscripts anymore, as I did for thirty years, nor do I claim to be an infallible reader of them. If I don't put my best energies into the fragile little business, I will surely lose—for myself, my partner, my staff, the authors we publish—the whole show. No, I do not owe that close reading and the thoughtful rejection note even to others who write, as I once did, to fill a terrible hunger in their hearts. I only owe to my business the best books I can find.

But I will say this: after the metamorphosis from supplicant author to tyrant publisher capable of administering the sternest judgment by rejection, I cannot help looking, myself, at every scrap of paper that comes my way from whatever source. I look a little or a lot, and I try to find some frank helpful thing to say— if only a few words or a pointing in another direction or the encouragement to work longer, harder—about every manuscript that heads back to its origins. I do not do so out of any obligation other than the selfish one: I keep thinking that something of value, of specific value to readers as well as to my publishing firm, will be there—and rooting around in such unsolicited manuscripts from people unknown to me I once found W. D. Wetherell's *Vermont River* and, not long ago, an autobiographical memoir by Robert Mengel, submitted by his widow. The title was a cliché, the author unknown to me, and I have already noted the plethora of fishing memoirs. I'd make short shrift of this one. But this book drew me in, and I smiled and traveled with the man and found—from the first paragraph on to the end—a person of intelligence and wit, a happy capacity for simple joys, a shrewd eye for the natural world (I later found out that he was a renowned ornithologist), and I grabbed it and published it as *Fly Fisherman's Odyssey*.

How then to decide?

However much I might enjoy bullhead fishing, I'd probably never publish a book on the subject. There are probably more bullheaders—wet and dry—than fly fishers, but do they read as much about their sport, and is there as much to say? But with the encouragement of a wise friend, I published *French Fishing Flies* some years ago—despite jeers and doubts that anyone cared about how the French did it—because there was no mention of French flies in the American fly tier's dialogues and there ought to have been. A steady diet of such books would bankrupt any publisher, but the book seemed important to me; it got few reviews and barely sold out a small first printing—but now everyone and his brother thinks he, independently, discovered *cul de canard.*

I've got to balance the books that will "earn out" soon and those that may pay for themselves in two, three, or even five years; I like to publish books that will stay in print that long or five times that long. I've got to balance a season's publications so that I don't have too many books competing in a narrow field; I could not publish Lee Wulff's book on Atlantic salmon and Gary Anderson's in the same season, so, much as I liked the latter, I let it go. I can't publish too many expensive or complicated books in a given season because I have neither the capital nor the personnel to do so (I'm the only person in my office who knows that *Paraleptophlebia* is not a foot fungus). I try to remember that a book is a book, not a "product" or a gimmick; that it ought to have a voice of its own, which is not its editor's voice or the Universal Time–Life Bland; that it ought to have something significant, new, or better to say; that it ought to be built to last a couple of years.

I actually like to publish very specialized books—books with what I call "special knowledge," such as *French Fishing Flies,* Darrel Martin's esoteric *Fly-Tying Methods* and *Micropatterns,* and *Dyeing and Bleaching Natural Fly-Tying Materials,* by A. K. Best. I'd love to do an American book on trout-stream plants, like the fine one on British plants by Macer Wright. I like to publish some regional books, if that region, like West Yellowstone, gets a large influx of visitors from other parts of the country, or has broader historical significance, like the Catskills of Mac Francis's brilliant book. I once listened to a long pitch by the author of a book about fishing in Tasmania; he swore that it was mathematically impossible not to sell ten thousand copies in the States, minimum, and I was tempted to publish it so I could do the editing over there but turned it back because my best common sense told me its maximum sale here was 427 copies.

I decided not to publish a book on Ogden Pleissner's paintings, though I like them a lot, because we simply have not got the expertise to produce books of the quality that one needed, nor could we invest that much of our limited capital in one book. (Another publisher brought this one out quite successfully.)

I have refused to publish books by people I didn't want to deal with (since publishing is a personal process as I practice it, and I'm careful about whom I climb into bed with); I have refused to publish books by people whose facts were bogus— or thirdhand; by people who never even learned the rudiments of writing; by people who have written a couple of articles and think the world is waiting to have their random comments bound in hardcover; by people who want to expand a decent little article into a book-length manuscript; by people who are writing about aspects of fishing that do not fascinate me—like snagging and woolly-buggering; by people whose books are not *quite* good enough, in an increasingly crowded field; by people who have *some* good ideas but not enough; by people who have written books I like but cannot publish if I do not want to lose "the use of my name for the rest of my life."

And, alas, I *have* published a liberal number of the above, too. Their presence in the world hurts me almost as much as the ones I rejected that I wish I hadn't. Both are sure emblems of any publisher's many flaws and fallibilities, in a field where a .500 batting average is probably as rare and strong as it is in baseball. And I have failed miserably, after ten years of trying, to get the best fly fisherman I know, and an excellent writer, to complete a book of compact essays on his genuinely unique experience.

I decided not to reprint several fly-fishing books first published by other houses because I thought that they were poorly conceived or that there were enough copies of the first edition available or that the books somehow lacked the capacity to last. It's hard to bring books, like Lazarus, back from oblivion and though I was happily able to do so with Flick and Marinaro

Modern Saltwater Sportfishing, Frank Woolner
Modern Tackle Craft, C. Boyd Pfeiffer
Montana Time, John Barsness
My Moby Dick, William Humphrey
Notes from the San Juans, Steven J. Meyers
Nymph Fishing for Larger Trout, Charles E. Brooks
Nymphs and the Trout, Frank Sawyer (I)
Opening Day and Other Neuroses, William G. Tapply
The Origins of Angling, John McDonald (R)
The Orvis Fly-Fishing Guide, Tom Rosenbauer
The Orvis Guide to Beginning Fly Tying, Eric Leiser
The Orvis Guide to Saltwater Fly Fishing, Nick Curcione
Power Surfcasting, Ron Arra with Curt Garfield
Practical Black Bass Fishing, Mark Sosin and Bill Dance
The Practical Fisherman, C. Boyd Pfeiffer
Practical Fishing Knots, Mark Sosin and Lefty Kreh
The Practical Fly Fisherman, A. J. McClane (R)
Practical Light Tackle Fishing, Mark Sosin
Prey, Carl Richards
Reading Trout Streams, Tom Rosenbauer
Return to the River, Roderick L. Haig-Brown (R)
A River Never Sleeps, Roderick L. Haig-Brown (R)
Rivers of the Heart, Steve Raymond
Saltwater Fly-Fishing Magic, Neal and Linda Rogers (D)
Saltwater Fly Patterns, Lefty Kreh (Rev)
Saltwater Fly Tying, Frank Wentink
San Juan River Chronicle, Steven J. Meyers
Selective Trout, Doug Swisher and Carl Richards
Silver, Roderick L. Haig-Brown (Rev)
Silver Swimmer, Richard Buck
Speycasting, Hugh Falkus (I)
The Sports Afield Fishing Almanac, Frank S. Golad (ed.)
The Sports Afield Treasury of Trout Fishing, Tom Paugh (ed.)
Sportsman's Legacy, William G. Tapply
Steelhead Country, Steve Raymond

Steelhead Fly Fishing, Trey Combs
Stillwater Trout, John Merwin (ed.)
Stoneflies, Doug Swisher, Carl Richards, and Fred Arbona
Stonefly and Caddis Fly Fishing, Leonard M. Wright, Jr.
The Stream Conservation Handbook, J. Michael Migel (ed.)
Streamer-Fly Fishing, John Merwin
The Striped Bass, Nick Karas (Rev)
A Summer on the Test, John Waller Hills (I)
The Sunfishes, Jack Ellis (D)
Superior Flies, Leonard M. Wright, Jr.
Lou Tabory's Guide to Saltwater Baits and Their Imitations,
   Lou Tabory
Tackle Care, C. Boyd Pfeiffer
Tackle Craft, C. Boyd Pfeiffer
Talleur's Dry-Fly Handbook, Dick Talleur
Tarpon Quest, John N. Cole
Thy Rod and Thy Creel, Odell Shepard (R)
To Know a River, Roderick L. Haig-Brown
Trout Biology, Bill Willers (Rev)
The Trout and the Fly, John Goddard and Brian Clarke (I)
Trout Magic, Robert Traver
Trout on a Fly, Lee Wulff
The Trout and the Stream, Charles E. Brooks
Trout Maverick, Leonard M. Wright, Jr.
Trout Stream Insects, Dick Pobst
Vermont River, W. D. Wetherell
The Versatile Fly Tyer, Dick Talleur
Wade a Little Deeper, Dear, Gwen Cooper and Evelyn Haas
   (Rev)
The Ways of Trout, Leonard M. Wright, Jr.
A Wedding Gift and Other Angling Stories, John Taintor Foote
   (Rev)
Western Fly-Fishing Strategies, Craig Mathews
What the Trout Said, Datus Proper (Rev)
Where the Bright Waters Meet, Harry Plunkett-Greene (I)

Dave Whitlock's Guide to Aquatic Trout Foods, Dave Whitlock
The Winchester Press Fish-Finding Guide, Leonard M.
   Wright, Jr.
Joan Wulff's Fly Casting Techniques, Joan Wulff
The Yellowstone Fly-Fishing Guide, Craig Mathews and Clayton
   Molinero
You Should Have Been Here Yesterday, John Troy

6 THE COLLECTOR'S BUG

I did not consciously become a "collector." People who love
books inevitably *collect* them. What starts as "accumulation"
graduates to "library" and settles into "collection."

   I began purely as an accumulator—bringing home books I'd
edited for Crown, adding old books I bought to consider for
republication, finding others in yard sales and library sales that
merely looked interesting, and buying those—used and new—
that had information I sorely wanted. The world of fly fishing
was mysterious and compelling, on and off the river, and I simply could not fish often enough, read enough about it.

   I kept the books in no special order, sandwiched my reading of them between Yeats, Whitman, and Melville, barely knew
what I had, and ended with six or seven hundred, some very
fine. Not much of it was "literature," but the best of it was full
of an earthy, practical knowledge, born of many days on the
water by observant and skillful folk; and the stories and theory
had a simple concreteness devoid of precisely the factitious
literary and academic pretensions I increasingly disliked.

   At first I mostly acquired lower-priced books selectively, in
the best copies I could find; I bought what could teach me what
I needed to know, about casting, Quill Gordons, and what I
thought I would enjoy. I had always liked to read everything
by an author when I started in with one—Jack London, Steinbeck, Hemingway, Faulkner, Kafka, and then half a hundred

others, so I accumulated all of Haig-Brown and everything I could find (and afford) by Mr. Skues, and then the same with Hewitt, LaBranche, Halford. This way I felt closer to an author, saturated with his best and worst.

Fly fishing requires mastery of a thousand skills—and specific needs call for specific, practical books. I learned knots from books, local and then national entomology, stream tactics, and much else. But I was tugged constantly to the vast world beyond the Quill Gordons and nail knots, for fly fishing had a long history, its own canon of classics, an astonishingly broad diversity (in both quality and range), and sheer numbers of different titles that, I saw, could lead to hopeless confusion—or a lifetime of reading and collecting. And to compound the problem, new books were being published in unprecedented numbers—and I was one of the culprits. Some recorded or advanced the state of the sport and provided the language modern sportsmen use; some conveyed practical information, developed new theories of trout behavior and fly construction, or provided pure pleasure. A lot simply muddied the waters.

After a few years I accelerated my acquisitions—unable to pass up a Salvation Army outlet, library sale, antique shop with books, rummage sale, street stall, or even a remainder table. The sporting field responds quickly to the pressure of high demand and low availability; I know of a half dozen cases within the past five years when remaindered books became worth double their list price a year after being abandoned by their not-so-knowledgeable publishers.

I didn't collect for "value," but I became aware of the issue by subscribing to the catalogs of Judith Bowman, the late Col. Henry Siegel (Anglers' and Shooters' Bookshelf), Kenneth Callahan, Gary Estabrook, Alec Jackson, and half a dozen others; and my son Tony, a dealer since his teens, instructed me. Reliable specialty dealers rather than random looking became my best single source for specific needs. They knew the field well; they could advise on variant editions; they could be trusted for quality; and they could often find what I needed, even when they did not have it in stock. A good dealer's catalog, in fact, became an education in value—though the latest prices yielded at an auction showed interesting variations. And there was also variation in the prices in different dealers' catalogs. A good dealer will describe books carefully, will ship them well packaged, and will advise honorably on a variety of practical matters associated with used and rare sporting books. A dealer who once ships you an ugly, ungainly edition with foxing, loose pages, and even disfiguration—none of which were noted in the catalog copy—should probably never be trusted again.

I didn't realize quite how attached I had become to my fishing books until I sold them. Most book collectors I've known have, at one time or another, sold all or part of their collection. What they've brought together with sweet passion, what has come to them by chance or gift or shrewd search or bid or bargaining leaves them in desperation. They need the money.

That's what happened to me. I had built a modest but unique angling-book collection. Since I write in the field and on occasion review, but mostly because I have made a little reputation as an editor of better fly-fishing books, a hundred copies of newer books were warmly inscribed to me; the rest I had bought during two decades of search, from thrift shops to yard and estate sales to used-book shops here and in England. They were good books, in excellent condition, dating back to 1820. Some, I knew, had substantial value.

When my four children were simultaneously attending college I accelerated an already manic schedule. I was holding down three jobs and ghostwriting, but the latter brought me not financial relief but a tax bill so large I had to arrange a last possible loan to pay it down. And the next year the tuitions were higher still. New York can take and take. Our rent skyrocketed, we had a few uninsured health problems—and I was exhausted, bewildered, and drained. I could pull the children out of college—and they would have understood—or I could sell something. My bamboo fly rods went first, but didn't bring much. I sold some rare flies. My extensive correspondence went to the late Bob Buckmaster (with the stipulation that it would all go, eventually, to the American Museum of Fly Fishing—where it now is). The books were worth the most and Tony had been selling sporting books for four years—and had real talent for it. He had a large customer list and produced a handsome catalog.

In the end I told him to describe and price them all, every last one of them, and sell them through his catalog. He'd take 20 percent, which he could use at college, and I *might* earn enough to keep everyone else in place and stay afloat. No one else in the family was to know. Tony catalogued every book, slowly and steadily, but stopped at the last one, standing prominently on the mantelpiece.

"Even the Sparse?" Tony asked.

I hesitated. "That too."

"The Sparse" was a unique copy of a book I had published eight years earlier. I had bet Alfred W. Miller, the brilliant curmudgeon, then in his late seventies, who wrote under the name of Sparse Grey Hackle, that Crown would go back to press for a second printing of his *Fishless Days, Angling Nights* by Christmas; we had published five thousand copies of the book in September, which he said was a ludicrously high number. This was his first trade book, and he had almost persuaded me to include a unique *descending* scale of royalties, which would encourage the publishing house to keep the book in print. Crown was willing—just as they had pressed for a *lead* binding to Flick's streamside guide; but I wouldn't allow either. The old guy had put together an exceptional book, one that would last on its own merits. I insisted that there would be no trouble keeping it in print for twenty years—and I was right.

"Okay, ten cents, Bub," he said. "That's my limit." He liked to punctuate with "Bub," or "Buster," or "Mister."

I agreed, we shook, and the deal was struck. Two months later we rushed through a second printing in time for Christmas. And a week later I pounded on a lunch table and demanded my dime.

"You'll get it," he growled. "You'll get it. I always pay my debts."

But he hadn't paid up by February, and I began to dun him mercilessly—by letter, by phone, via mutual friends, whenever I saw him. He only smiled, squinted, chewed on his pipe, and acknowledged that he owed me the dime and that it was a lot of money but I'd get it.

In April he came into my office—with his pin-striped suit, vest, half-inch-thick glasses, cane, and sparse scalp, looking like a gnome or a tax collector—and summarily dropped a package on my desk. "I always pay my debts, Mister," he said, and then turned and scuffled out.

"Yes, Tony," I said, eight years later, "hold back nothing. Sell it all. 'The Sparse,' too."

What Sparse had given me was a copy of *Fishless Days, Angling Nights* bound in green Nigerian goatskin, with raised hubs, handsome gold-leaf scrollwork and design, and marbled endpapers. Stamped in gold on the face of the cover were the words, "For Nick, who made this book."

Above the words, the binder had inset in the leather, with gold dots circling it, a silver dime, well polished. On the front endpaper was a long, very personal inscription.

"Charge a lot for it, Tony," I said, perhaps hoping it would not sell, or hoping that something valuable to me would not necessarily be valuable to someone else. In fact, a few dealers laughed at the price, $750, and advised Tony that it was only a regular trade edition, with the same paper and some value added on. I had to agree.

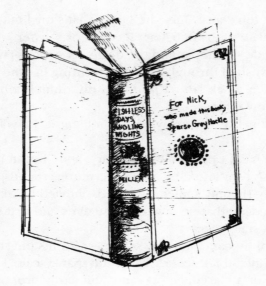

Tony, whose will is iron, said simply, "That's the price; if you don't want it, just don't buy it."

In fact, it sold soon, at exactly that price, and we sold out most of the rest of the collection quickly, too, saving my skin. I was never again in such a financial slough and when I could I began to collect again, with even more care and determination.

I heard twice that the Sparse book had come up for sale and had sold for somewhat more than the $750, but took only a mild interest, forgot, recalled a little, forgot again. It had happened many busy years earlier. Then a few winters ago, when I saw it listed in an auction catalog, I remembered everything and immediately called several dealers to ask them to bid for me. The prices they thought it would fetch, though, were beyond my reach and one said that "everyone" was interested in the book.

Tony had just finished law school, was living at home, and when he saw the listing, said: "Dad, we've got to buy it." We agreed to split the price and planned our trip.

The listing, in fact, was of that embarrassing brand that tells all: the inscription in gold; the inscription by Sparse inside, explaining why he had given me the dime and other flattering stuff, and my letter, written by request to the first buyer, telling him the whole story behind the book, in somewhat prolix fashion.

Though the weather report held snow warnings, I agreed to drive upcountry with Tony, his girlfriend, Helena, and Mari. I had never bid before and Tony had, but we decided that the top figure we'd go to was $2,500. Several of the dealers said that they had refused to bid for their clients because I was bidding; I told them this was not necessary. Several others said they would bid. Everyone appeared to be talking about that book. Then, just minutes before the auction began, one dealer drew me outside to tell me a confidential story. Tony, standing next to me, came too. The story was this: in the men's room, he had stood next to a fellow whom he knew slightly; he had asked the man what he intended to buy. The man mentioned ten or twelve books and then said, "*Fishless Days, Angling Nights;* that's what I really want." The dealer said he told the fellow that I had come and was apparently anxious to get it back—and the fellow said that that didn't bother him: he was going to get it, no matter what. At least that's what I was told.

All right, I thought, it's an open auction. Someone is selling and he's entitled to the price the room will deliver. I shrugged, said, "What can I say," and turned to walk inside, where the auction was ready to begin. Tony said nothing. He is a big young man—six foot three, built like a football player or a weight lifter, still with every bit of that will he had as a boy, and a shrewd knowledge of book values. We sat together for a half hour, in the front, listening to the books come and go, and then I decided to stand in the center, in the back, where I could watch—and perhaps learn how to do this thing. I saw some dealers hesitate and then come back; others came in full force at once; I saw everyone in the room hold back . . . and then bid a book up to three times its expected value. I saw a few people slow-ing matters down when the bidding went too fast. And I saw a man bidding aggressively and taking a large portion of the books.

It is one thing to observe and understand *timing,* another to have it. I had it in basketball and now have it, physically, in fly fishing. For many years I had every last bit of it in the class-room, teaching without notes, closely attached to my students. I had never bid for anything, anywhere. The bidding for the Sparse book started at $1,200 (below the price it had last sold for) and within seconds went to $1,800. A few dealers put in early bids, then only two of us remained. I had kept my hand up all the time, innocently thinking that this was the best of the strategies I'd seen; let him know, and it *was* the man who had been buying so many books, that I'm in the game to win. But he would glance over at me, smile—ironically, I thought—and raise his hand slowly after each of my bids. I had lost all rhythm and we were both caught in some of that mad emo-tional music that I have seen cause great businesses and bid-ders to go bust. At least I was.

I said yes to nineteen; he went to two thousand.

I said twenty-one.

He said yes at twenty-two.

I said twenty-three.

He half turned and said twenty-four.

I quickly said twenty-five, my last bid.

Deliberately—and smiling again—he said yes to twenty-six.

There was a moment of utter silence. Not even the auction-eer moved.

Tony looked straight at me from the front row. I shook my head. It had been fair bidding. The man had more money. I had already bid ten times more than I had ever paid for a book. I'd gone up quickly. I should have waited.

"Going once," the auctioneer said. "Twice."

And then Tony's long arm rose powerfully to its full length, hand open like a pancake. He kept it there. He meant it. What was he doing? How high did he intend to go? The room was stone silent. My opponent looked, blinked—may have seen Tony as a new, erratic, wealthy bidder who could take the game anywhere . . . and he shook his head. The room burst from silence to applause.

Tony stood right up and circled to the cashier, where he quickly wrote a check, collected the book, and walked slowly and directly toward me, then handed me "The Sparse."

An hour later, racing to beat the worst of the snowstorm that was just starting, Tony, from the driver's seat, said, "I don't have the slightest idea what it's worth . . . but I'm glad we got it."

And a few moments later, leaning over to say the words in his ear, I said, "Me, too."

"And it's worth exactly what we paid for it, Dad. That's what it was worth to us today. Tomorrow it'll be worth five grand . . ."

"More!"

"No one will have enough to buy it!"

"Well," said Mari, quite silent through all this male bonding, "that's the first time I've seen a dime sell for two thousand seven hundred dollars."

"It was worth every penny," said Tony.

"You two are crazy . . ."

"That was beautiful," said Helena.

"For a dime? Two thou—"

"Mom!" said Tony.

"It could have been worse," I said, quietly hugging her in the back seat like we'd hugged when we first found each other, thirty-seven years ago, before kids, cities, and financial sloughs. I chose not to tell her about the buyer's premium.

"I don't see how," she said and kissed me as we fled home— one of my arms wrapped around my wife, the other around the book Sparse made for me.

7 THE HEART OF BOOKS

What is well-wrought lasts—and lasts. What is cheap trivializes the sport, gives ammunition to the opponents of sport, and wraps coffee grounds the next day.

I don't have the specific copies of the books that infected the dreams of this city boy with the stillness and wildness of the natural world, the essence of fishing. They barely survived the old coal room in our Brooklyn basement, and my mother must have thrown them out after my stepfather left her and she moved into a small L-shaped apartment in Manhattan. I'd like to have them, the exact copies, but I have had to settle for the words, which I still go back to, fifty years later. I still find great satisfaction in Ray Bergman, Howard Walden, and Roderick Haig-Brown. What they wrote was well wrought—and it lasts and lasts.

Before I bought back Sparse's book, and more assiduously since then, I had become a serious collector of books, of my own stripe—for collecting is the most personal of activities, as sure a totem of one's individuality as a fingerprint.

The best collections—of anything from Chinese porcelain to nineteenth-century trout flies—are built by those who have a discerning eye (for both the object itself and the right dealer to work with) and enough money in the bank to buy the best: the most important and valuable books in the best condition. Such collectors can pay for the best advice and pay for the rarest, most expensive books. Perhaps as important is the principle that animates a collection—and its relationship to one's life. I know one man who, for twenty years, has sought to collect merely *every* fly-fishing book published. He has a speculator collection, carefully housed, carefully cataloged, and it is clearly one of the great passions of his life. He has bought several major collections, merged them, sold off absolute duplicates, kept every possible variation in printing and binding. He used to spend several weeks of every year looking for new titles in England; he receives virtually every sporting-book catalog; he wants every variant edition of a book; he constantly upgrades what he has with finer copies of any title. The man clearly has the wherewithal to pursue such a major passion—and his collection, the mere listing of which takes some eight hundred pages, is greater than the combined collections of fishing books in the British Museum, the libraries at Harvard, Princeton, and Yale, and the great New York Public Library, and a dozen clubs and museums.

Another friend sold his general collection and now collects only editions of *The Compleat Angler,* of which he has four hundred and fifty or so. Still others would find a lot of Walton hard to swallow and strive to collect a balanced, intelligent group of four or five hundred of the best books only—and completely ignore insignificant titles.

I now collect chiefly what I want to read, in the best edition I can find, and I want to read what feeds some particular aspect of my passion at a given time—trout-vision, entomology, casting, dry-fly design, theory, bass, saltwater, chalkstream tactics; I buy every fly-fishing book of "literary" value that I hear about —though I often trade off the ones I'm sure I'll never read again. There's a dreadful plethora of sheer incompetence and bilge.

I have become especially interested in the language used by a handful of major writers (of novels or distinguished nonfiction)—writers like John Graves, Thomas McGuane, and, earlier, Hemingway. I have talked about language with John Graves, and we have debated particularly the use of language understood chiefly by serious practitioners of the sport: 6X leaders, Tricos, reach casts, *Paraleptophlebias,* fast action, drag, and so much else. At worst it is jargon; at best it borders on jargon. Few serious readers who do not fish can understand a word of it. Graves wisely says he wants language that can be understood by the best general reader; McGuane and Hemingway embody such a principle. But I, stubbornly, and at a much lower level of skill, insist upon the most intimately technical language possible; I am a fishing writer, not a writer who fishes. I like those technical words as much as Balzac likes the technical printing words in *Lost Illusions*—and I find the writing of the best writers irresistible, collectible, and quite beyond my ken.

I want a library that is coherent, helpful, interesting, with books I can use for reference, that I will return to frequently, for advice, to make friends with, to live in. I'm acutely aware of value now—but should I acquire a valuable book that I don't especially want to keep I'll often use it in trade. I horse trade a lot, mostly with a few dealers, not because I'm especially good at it—which I'm not—but because more books come through my hands than cash and they are one way I can keep my library-collection growing. All of the dealers have want lists from me; all know I cannot buy in the highest financial categories.

Books lead to books. A lot of leads on what I want to add come from references in other books. Two of Arnold Gingrich's books, *The Joys of Trout* and *The Fishing in Print*, provide shrewd judgments on the value of significant angling literature. You cannot read Gingrich (who, rather charmingly, was a shameless name dropper) without wanting to read some of his favorites—A. J. McClane, Charles Ritz, Preston Jennings, Odell Shepard, and that delicious ichthyologist Brian Curtis. He didn't recommend *Golden Days* by Romilly Fedden, *Where the Bright Waters Meet* by Harry Plunkett-Greene, *Fishing a Highland Stream* by John Inglis Hall, or *A Man May Fish* by T. C. Kingsmill-Moore; they came from friends whose judgment I trust, in the middle of sentences, randomly. They stayed in my library, for better or worse, because of my judgments. Ultimately, everything depends on that, doesn't it? Choice. What one chooses defines almost as sharply as what one makes.

When a supercilious retriever asks that marvelous bull terrier Trub, in *Trub's Diary* by John Taintor Foote, what he does best, Trub truthfully replies: "Eat and chase cats." A moment comes when he invades the premises of two ladies who keep scores of cats. At first he can hardly believe his good fortune. "Cats," Trub recalls, "began going in every direction. They went up the backs of chairs. They went up curtains. They went round and round the room. I thought: 'This is the life!' But it wasn't. You can't chase ten or twelve cats at once. I had an idea. It came to me in a quick way. The idea was 'Pick a cat!'"

It's a useful concept for those who love books, of which there are far too many. We must pick carefully when we start to collect or we will be chasing so many goals we'll miss the pleasure of catching any.

Intelligence determines value, the marketplace determines price. I saw a special "super"-limited edition of Preston Jennings's *A Book of Trout Flies* (Derrydale, a low-numbered copy of the edition of twenty-five copies, with a matched box containing a full set of flies tied by the author) sell for $12,500 at a Christie's auction; less than a year later, I saw a better copy, with a lower number, sell for $7,500 at another auction house. Why? There was simply not another person in the room to push the price up. I had stood next to the man at Christie's and if ever I saw a man determined to get something, at any cost, it was him: he'd have paid $50,000 for that book.

I have very handsome copies of Norman Maclean's *A River Runs Through It* today—and try not to think that, as one of the first reviewers of that great book I once had two sets of bound galleys and gave them both to forgotten friends, along with four first editions I promptly bought, because I like to share. They're worth a small fortune now.

The condition of the book affects the price absolutely; the edition is important (and in some cases, like Alfred Ronalds's *The Fly-Fisher's Entomology,* a later edition is more valuable than a first); the importance of the book counts; and of course anything like personal letters from the author, or a signature, or a long inscription (and to whom—association value) will help push up the price. Always the number printed is a factor; the Derrydale Press editions were all limited press runs, and since they were generally carefully selected books and handsomely produced volumes, they're prized collector's items in the sporting field. But some trade editions were quite small, and this affects price, too; Vincent Marinaro's *A Modern Dry-Fly Code* was originally printed in an edition of about one thousand, and though it was published in 1950 it's now worth more than $150. An intriguing postscript is that the book was remaindered and I know several people who bought up a dozen or more for about a buck apiece. Price always responds to the pressure of high demand and low availability.

But the building of a collection is more than the building of something personal and valuable; in angling, it is the participation in something much larger. For no sport lives daily in its heritage more intimately than fly fishing for trout. When a trout rises to our no-hackle we are linked, instantly, to a trout rising to one of Dame Juliana's flies, which also lacked hackle; our concerns for approach, presentation, imitation, stream reading, propriety, good fellowship, and angling values grow out of and are yet linked to like concerns by fly fishers who fished fifty, one hundred, two hundred years ago. We fish more deeply and more meaningfully in the present if we have understood the past—and, in its books, fly fishing has an incomparably textured and richly diverse past. And if we come to know this past and love it, and represent it on shelves in our homes, and live at least with respect for the traditions that grow from it, we inevitably want to protect not only them but the waters that make them possible. There is a subtle and seamless web that joins all life in the rivers we fish—and there is an equally complex web of relationships in the life and spirit and mores and technology of the books about them.

My passion for collecting fly-fishing books, which bloomed in two installments, appears not to be exhaustible in my lifetime. It is a passion that has led inescapably from my first primitive days of accumulating books to a defined sense of the library

I wanted, to a sense of this thing outside of me—these shelves of my study, filled with books I've chosen—as my collection. The passion still leads me to check every garage sale, every rummage, library, and block sale, every used-book store I've ever entered; it is a passion that leads me into correspondence with thoughtful dealers in every part of the country, with other collectors; it is connected to monetary value but not dependent upon it for the deepest pleasures I take from my books; it is filled with dramatic discoveries and the relaxed pleasures, late at night, of returning to favorite passages, old friends, on my bookshelves. And I am growing to love the skills of bookmaking itself, late, and as something not in opposition, as a fetish (as I once thought) to the words of the books, which chiefly drew me to write and publish and collect. Mostly, though, collecting fly-fishing books enables me to explore rivers I will never fish, explore theories and practices that give great pleasure in themselves and cannot help but affect next season's sport, and live for a while in another fly fisher's boots, brain, and heart.

SPHINX MOUNTAIN
AND BROWN TROUT

The landscape lives in me.
—PAUL CÉZANNE

Art is a sphinx. The beauty of the sphinx is that
you yourself must do the interpreting. When you
have found an interpretation, you are already cured.
The mistake people make is to believe that the
sphinx can give only one answer. Actually, it
gives hundred of answers, or maybe none at all.
Interpretation probably does not give us the truth,
but the act of interpretation saves us.
—SAUL STEINBERG
(Quoted by Pierre Schneider in *Louvre Dialogues*)

1 FROM THE BENCH

A landscape is a state of mind.
—HENRI FREDERIC AMIEL

From the house on the bench, I can see Sphinx Mountain rise
from a low section of the Madison Range like a gargantuan
stump, rudely cut. It is the farthest solid thing across the lush

bottomland, beyond the ribbon that is the Madison River, cobalt blue between the cottonwoods; now and then, on a bright morning, with the sun rising beyond it, the river is polished silver. Beyond the river there is another bench, then the sloping foothills, then the strange mountain itself, fourth in line from the north, after Lone, Fan, and Cedar. Today there is a solid pack of snow in what appears to be its concave top, veins of white in the front crevice, a washboard grid of snow on the left side, with palisades above. We have been here for two weeks and I have never seen this particular Sphinx. Today it seems cupped at the top, like a vessel about to receive something, though I don't think anyone upstairs is handing anything out lately, if in fact he hasn't departed to other worlds, we having made a mess of things here. But there is little mess from the bench—a couple of wood or metal bridges, jackleg fence posts, a bit of barbed wire, this cedar home.

As we drove along the rutted dirt road from Ennis the first day of our summer visit, it was at first not visible, then partially visible, then visibly different each moment, constantly changing into a procession of configurations and colors. It seems in perpetual motion, like Montana clouds, symbols of mutability. In various lights it was variously different—now dark green at its base from pines that seem to weld it to the rising hills; now Payne's gray at its rocky summit, or slate gray, or purple, or white, or pink, or ochre—or, yesterday afternoon, tawny red. The earth's anatomy is exposed here—sinew and bone of what holds it, the trees a skin. Some folks in town say they used to call it Red Mountain or Brick Top; someone said it once looked like a Sphinx, but a piece fell off. No one knows exactly when people started to call it that.

Several times I woke early, about five, and sat naked at the window watching the emergence of the sun; at first the top of the Sphinx is not there and I must take it on trust that it still *is* because it was. It is *always* there, I must remind myself, even when it is not visible; what matters matters, whether it's perceived or not. Then, inchmeal, it incarnates, as the brightening behind the dun-gray clouds allows it to become itself, and then suddenly the sun and mountain are so bright that, for a moment, I must look away. And sometimes in the evenings, with the infection of light from the sunset in the west, above the Gravellies, it is a dozen gaudy reds and purples, even bright crimson, as if it contains fire, as in a Turner. And sometimes it is merely a silhouette, a cutout, a straight man to the sky—black clouds, pink light, streaks of blue.

The mountain changes as you look at it, and it changes radically as we drive south on Route 287 toward West Yellowstone, or float the river, or wander down along the Madison Valley bottomland. Two miles south and that structure in front, called the Helmet, begins to walk away and we can see clearly that there are two mountains, not one, substantially apart. In a photograph my friends Lester and Ann, from Big Sky, sent me, of the other side of the mountain, it bears no resemblance to what my eyes tell me it is from the bench; my son Paul, standing on the narrow ledge at its summit, looked out for fifty miles in all directions along the Madison River but saw little of the thing he stood upon.

Wandering and changing as it does the mountain makes me think of Melville's whale, ubiquitous in time and space, here, there, spotted in several places at the same time, well out of water here in the Rockies.

But this heap of stone is dead. It does not breathe, does not seek anyone; nor is it sought for oil or vengeance, though the land-sellers have begun to hawk its image. It is merely there in front of us, big as life, solid as a fire in a cave in the Caucasus, different on Tuesday after the high snows came, and ten minutes ago, now that the snow is melting, perfectly indifferent to my eyes, without inherent meaning, dumb as a stone—a mass of reddish rock, coarse gravel, and red sand eponymously called

Sphinx conglomerate, originally under water then formed seventy million years ago. And even now this anchor of the landscape is not quite fixed. Gradually, it has been forced upward by geological forces similar to those that caused the huge earthquake forty miles south in 1959. Some geologists claim it still grows by as much as two inches a year.

I am not a geologist and can never know more than a fraction of its life—not even what they mean when they say it is "clearly contemporaneous with Laramide regional deformation," which sounds like art criticism—and that second- or thirdhand. But I am here on the bench and it is always there, across the valley, and it intrigues me and it has been trying for some weeks to wedge itself into my brain, become more than it is—though of course it is I who am trying to make a heap of rock become more than it is, and I have to remember Freud's observation that sometimes a cigar is just a cigar. Still, Emerson says, "Every object rightly seen unlocks a quality of the soul," and this hunk is worth the looking, getting into my head.

Mari is here too, of course, and for her it simply begs to be painted. It is an object, like many others she has painted, that serves merely as an object from which to begin, like Cézanne's apples or his Mont Sainte-Victoire, which also are themselves and more. And it is various enough for her to view in many different ways. She has painted it from the valley, where I go to fish in a spring creek, from upriver and down, and from our house, directly across. It reminds her of Goya's architect—solid, proud, beyond mannerism and triviality—and Rembrandt's late self-portraits, and Mount Fuji, and Cézanne's mountain in Provence.

Today, from my table in the living room I watch Mari paint in the first tentative outline of the mountain. She is using a Mars brown and a thin brush. First I see the Sphinx, in front of me, in itself, emerge from the canvas steadily. Then there is blue, which is also sky, and strokes that are trees or fields or the far bench.

In two hours there are greens that might be cottonwoods, a dozen yellows and greens that are the valley that sits between our house and the river, with hints of blue flax and lupine. I see patches of cobalt blue, streaks of silver, and look beyond the canvas to a river, visible between the trees, the only moving thing in the landscape other than the hawk hunting above the field. What's on the canvas does not "depict" or "represent" but has become some strange new creature of its own. The rose brambles in front of me are not on the canvas, nor is the white-tailed deer in the valley, nor the hawk (now gone, anyway), nor a thousand other details. But those forms that are on the canvas could not exist without that other thing, the physical thing, beyond it. This that is on the canvas is not an emotional response either, an "echo of the soul"; nor is it romantic. I shall learn what it is, I promise myself.

I look at the woman now, tall and thin, her hair frizzy and blond, in a tank shirt and blue coveralls, separate from me now, caught in some triangle with landscape and canvas, and I can see what she sees (with my different eyes), and I can see that thing on the canvas, struggling to become itself. A camera would capture it all, all at once, the Sphinx at this moment, as it has been for the past few hours. The mountain will be different again before she stops painting for the day. There are great photographs and she knows it, but she tweaked the camera impishly yesterday when I suggested that it could anchor the scene for her, become a point of reference.

"Different mountain," she said. Then: "I love photographs as much as anyone, dear, especially if they're of our four children."

So, we have come to this spot to transact some private business—I to fish and write, Mari to put color and forms in water-color and oil paint on paper and canvas. We'll be here a month, maybe more, and perhaps we'll come back. We are not of this place but of a place that is a totem for placelessness, a city—a rootless nowhere, full of jewels. We both want a somewhere—but we are visitors here, and at this time of our lives it's now clear that we will never have such a place. This is not Walden Pond; we are not even here for a long visit. But we are here together, after a trip of nearly forty years' duration, over rocky

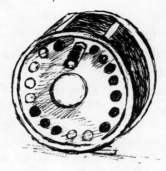

terrain, with four children, now grown. And this is a *place,* and the mountain is real—though it may well also be a state of mind.

My Underwood Standard, Model "S," vintage 1945, is on the table before me. I have transported to this place my heaps of books, notebooks, and paper; I have thirty years' worth and I need to organize them—and my life. I have my fly rods and innumerable boxes of flies stacked in the hallway. My boots and vest hang on nails just outside the front door.

I don't understand my passion for fishing, and especially for the brown trout, nor do I have to. But it is there, and Vaughan is due at the house in an hour to take us downriver.

Suddenly, that is immensely important to me.

2 RIVER HOURS

> Water, the image of the mind,
> clears as it runs, and as it runs, refines.
> —J. M. W. TURNER,
> in a speech on reflections

You can see the great mountain now and then as we float in the late afternoon on the Madison River—between the trees, across the fields, towering over the benches, here, then gone, but we have come for something else this time. The Sphinx is incidental, irrelevant.

When we first came to the Downing House three weeks ago, the giant stonefly had begun to hatch and all day, every day, cars towing driftboats rattled up and down the Varney Road, throwing dust. There were fifty-three of them one day and that was more than I cared to contend with. Floaters came down the ribbon of cobalt regularly and, because of the low willows, you could not always see the boat; sometimes it looked as if they were walking or sitting on water as they glided swiftly downriver. The river, which was high when we came, has been dropping by degrees; I walk to it every day, look over the Varney Bridge, watch the rocks appear with greater distinctness every day, a world more visible each hour the river clears. And as it clears, now and then, I can spot the wavering dark forms of the trout.

I fished it a few times from one of the access points and now, finally, I am floating with Vaughan Herrick, casting quickly to one bank or the other, watching a big fly float along the shadowline near the shore, where I've always found the largest fish. It is pleasant work. I stand in the front, leaning into the concave nose of the MacKenzie River boat, and watch the water come to me and watch for likely places to cast, perhaps a rising fish. There are absolutely no fish rising and I have had the odd feeling that their numbers have somehow diminished. There seem to be more birds. Earlier, an osprey dive-bombed the river with extended claws, smashing into the riffled surface and coming up with a two-pound rainbow trout, gleaming silver, still shaking as the great bird lifted off—one fish the better of me.

Mari does not fish but she is showing more interest in this intense dance of mine—the leaning forward, the hard look, the poised rod, the angle of the line being cast, the strike, the struggle. She is watching me at my play, and out of the corner of my eye I watch her. Several times when we stopped floating I merely sat back on a rock to her side and kept glancing at her working, the quick strokes of her watercolor brush—like a swallow inscribing a shadow on the flat surface of the creek—fixing an image on the paper, not the scene itself but some painted adumbration, some other world, separate and complete unto itself, hooked to the real one. Watercolor painting had been new to her when we first went west fifteen years ago, and at first she worked as if her medium were still oil paint, which she could paint over, rework, build, even as Albert Ryder worked his haunting scenes into brooding layers of darkness. Watercolor was quick and final.

But on the river, my eyes always returned to moving water, with those great speckled mysteries holding somewhere in its depths. Then Mari vanished, the mountain was gone, and I was concerned only with how to get my fly into the long shadow against the shoreline, beyond the current seam, and how to manipulate the line and fly so that the fly would stay in that dark shadow and float naturally. This seemed a modest goal. It was not nearly like trying to get some fragment of the Montana landscape onto a piece of paper or canvas without competing with a camera or a realist. But though I was always up to my gills in the first, increasingly I realized how much I wanted to understand the other. For I love painting and for forty years, watching Mari's work evolve, it has been a deeper and deeper part of my life. She never quit, despite the indifference, the raw discouragement, even from closest friends—like Cézanne took it from Zola in *The Masterpiece*. She was never slick or satisfied; she looked, she struggled, she grew, and I loved her work, which had since I married her been entangled with my life.

At the end of the float I help Vaughan trailer the boat, and then he drives us back to the Downing House. Vaughan is quite tall, very straight; he has been in war and he has been in the war of business. Now he lives in Montana with his wife, Judy; they run a bed-and-breakfast near the house we've rented and

Vaughan guides on the river. He is very good at it—but after a long day, I have had only two fish on, one to my hand. I saw a few fish rise and felt a couple of ticks that might have been fish or rocks; Mari has made half a dozen sketches and she lays them out on the dining table and we look carefully at each. One is a happy little rendering of a boat going by; another is muddy and she summarily rips it up—for the act of making a water-color admits no possibility of revision, of the sort of tinkering Yeats or Flaubert were given to, fussing with a line for a week or a month, until the result seemed "a moment's thought." We once visited a famous watercolorist's studio and saw engraved into a beam a maxim: "Fixing a watercolor is like trying to change a lie: the more you try the worse it gets." There was a quick sketch of the brown I caught, animated, wavering in the water, sure-handed, and one from the back of the MacKenzie River boat, past Vaughan, who rowed, including the nose of the boat and a bit of me. At my weight I was glad she had not been able to record all of me in the sketch. There were two draw-ings that included the mysterious mountain, poking through the trees. That was the metamorphosis of it: a thing outside of her, with a life of its own, like a brown trout, finds its way into her notebooks and then, perhaps, becomes a painting, or, like the one of me and John Goddard, ends up on the cover of a book. Or, like the muddy sketch, it gets ripped. "I don't paint to keep from spoiling paper or canvas," she likes to say.

Mari's "fishing" had been better than mine, and it was better still when we tramped around Spring Creek a few days later, me fishing hard, she trailing me with pad, watching and sketching.

Mostly I forgot that she was there.

I fished up the familiar East Branch, knowing exactly how best to approach each pool, having a trim box of killing flies in my vest, the products of some mastery since, a decade earlier, I first blundered around this tough river. I enjoyed having developed the skills to fish here with some success. I took fish in the Middle Bend Pool and the Second Bend Pool and then, oblivious to all but the hypnotic tug of the river, I approached the Third Bend Pool. It was the smallest of the first pools on the East Branch, with a sharp center current, several braided currents, a full 120-degree turn, and, beyond the currents, a slack eddy the size of a child's wading pool. The trick, I'd learned a few years ago, was to fish up the left side, the outward rim of the current, and directly upstream into the slack water. Too many anglers tried to fish across the current; I'd given that up years ago. Best was to stand very quietly against the left bank, the slack water no more than thirty feet above, and wait. That's what I did and in a few moments I saw a bit of nervous water that, in another context, might have meant a tadpole or a small turtle. It wasn't much. But I'd seen such movement here before. I cast a small Elk-Hair Caddis up to where the water had flounced a bit and a great buster of a brown trout took the fly at once, raced powerfully upriver, came caterwauling out of the water and crashing back, leaped again, and landed in a patch of thistle along the bank. "Ha!" I muttered, never having seen this before. For an instant I thought it might be trapped in the weeds, so I lifted myself onto the bank and prepared to race toward the great fish—perhaps six pounds of it—but the thrashing and flopping continued and

the trout was soon back in the water, leaving my fly a scarred bit of feathers among the nettles.

"Ahhhh," I said and turned to see if Mari had witnessed this dramatic clownishness.

But she was still sitting on the rim of the Middle Bend Pool, where I'd last seen her, an hour ago.

When I first hauled Mari to Montana decades ago to fish this perfectly remarkable spring creek, she went reluctantly. She hated to leave her studio for a month and thought her oils and canvases too cumbersome to take along. Also, after far too many years of it, she still found the endless fish-talk boring in the extreme and never tried to learn the difference between a *Hexagenia limbata* and a handsaw; and she still called my fly rods "poles."

But by the second year she began to work her way, increasingly, into the special demands of watercolor—and then, steadily, she began to work almost as long as I fished, which is a lot. She'd set up her portable easel, low to the ground and out of the wind, sit on the canvas bush chair she brought, and get to work at once, finding fixed points in the vast Montana landscape to paint over and over, especially that certain stump of a form on the horizon. Or she'd trail after me, sketching with a pen, sometimes brushing color into the sketches. When I finished *Spring Creek,* I found a watercolor of a man crouched

and casting that made a fine jacket, and I found forty line drawings that the publisher happily took for the interior; and then,
as I began to assemble the essays in *A Flyfisher's World,* and
the little book *My Secret Fish-Book Life,* I realized that I wanted
nothing more than to have our work commingled, and I realized too that she had finally found her connection to this odd
and enduring passion of mine for rivers and fly fishing, through
her work.

Once, on a cold and drizzly evening after I'd fished hard all day,
she insisted we go back to the river. I said I found it very comfortable in front of the fire, thank you, with a scotch in my hand.
She asked if I was sick or something and I reluctantly allowed
myself to be hauled down to the water. It was grayer and colder
by Spring Creek and I sat in the driver's seat, warmly dressed,
and took out a book while she started a small watercolor.

"You *are* sick, aren't you?" she said.

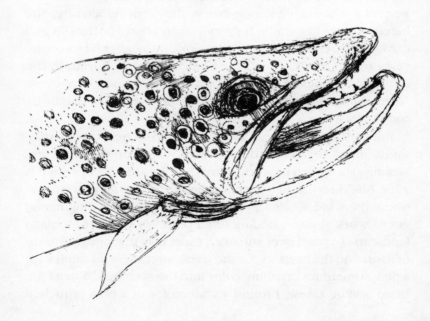

"Tired. Fished out," I said.

"That'll be the day."

"It's true."

"If you're not sick, get out of here and fish!" she said, and practically pushed me out of the car. I reluctantly took my rod down from the carrier on the roof of the Suburban, walked to the edge of the water, a vast pool, and shivered. I turned back to her and she pointed to a bright double rainbow near Sphinx Mountain. It probably looked better from the car, I thought, but I smiled pleasantly, shivered and shook a few times, looked across the dark, cold water, saw a robust snout poke up some forty feet out, and took it on my first cast, the largest brown I've ever taken, which she sketched before I turned it back.

And then I said: "Satisfied?"

"No."

"Then let's go back to bed, big girl."

3 TWO THOUSAND MILES FROM HERE

> O the mind, mind has mountains, cliffs of fall
> Frightful, sheer, no-man-fathomed.
> Hold them cheap
> May who ne'er hung there.
> —GERARD MANLEY HOPKINS

Two thousand miles from here, there is a great gray city, called "Mannahatta" by Whitman, parochial and worse by westerners I know. A dozen upcountry friends have been conned within minutes after they arrived at Grand Central Station, or blasted in the eyes by soot. One man would not get into a cab without an escort. In more than thirty-five years, I was mugged once, when a mob of kids surrounded Mari and I, one ripped off her necklace, and they scattered; and a quick hand got money from my pocket in the subway once. I try to keep three steps ahead of them now.

Two thousand miles from here, Mari has a large studio over H & H Bagels on Eightieth Street and Broadway. I think of her room often, with its hundreds and hundreds of paintings, books everywhere, still lifes with flowers, fruits, sculptor's props, and skulls she began to collect when her father, a California cattle dealer, sent her boxes labeled "Bones." And there are cityscapes, figure studies, dancers, early landscapes from the days we spent in Woodstock, and a great number of self-portraits, from all periods of her life. In the room, I must slip sideways through the maze of canvases; I like to see brushes held on corrugated cardboard, paints fresh on wax paper, work in various stages of incarnation, mirrors, paint-stained coveralls, photographs and prints pinned to bits of wall space, bottles of damar varnish and turpentine; I like the thick smell of oil paint.

These past few years there are also large landscapes, made from the sketches and drawings she does here in Montana, canvases up to a full seven by eight feet, perhaps fifty of them. When I enter this world I see the fullness of work, the mystery of art, a richness of spirit; but I have invited people to visit and they are overwhelmed by the sheer volume of color and form, the canvases stacked face out, one enjambed with another, the room often dominated by one current series, like the new paintings of Montana.

After the most difficult years with four infants, only five years separating the first and last, she rented that room on the third floor, sharing it with a succession of painters and finally taking it all for herself, about a thousand square feet of it. A year ago she stretched out even further and took a storage room, to leave herself more space to paint.

Before these paintings of the Montana landscape, she did an extended series of self-portraits, and before that she did cityscapes and still lifes—fifty or more of each. The self-portraits, she told me the other night when we were looking out at the silhouette of the Sphinx, lit by a quarter moon, began because she had a cheap model. But they became a searching in paint for an elusive selfhood—intense, questing, angry at the lack of certainty, in herself, in the world, in art. "My self-portraits," she said, "frighten people, I think—women as well as men. An angry woman painted by a man—Dubuffet, de Kooning, Picasso—is an icon; an angry woman painted by a woman is intimidating, is a hag."

"But they're not angry," I argued.

"They're serious—and that's worse. It makes people very nervous."

"Like Frida Kahlo?" I asked.

She thought for a moment and said: "Her problems don't interest me. They're gynecological. It's *her* situation as a woman and it's just not widely human. That's neurosis, not meaning. Some women show a vagina and it's a feminist statement of some kind."

In some of the self-portraits, the face—the seat of character—has been reworked fifty times, built up with brush and palette knife. This is a specific woman who thinks any woman, or man, is a complex piece of work, a dozen different people every hour, worth a closer look—not a symbol, not anecdotal, not a psychological laboratory, not a statement.

I think about the portraits a lot—though no one else seems to have thought twice about them. *The New York Times* reviewed some painted body bags a few floors below her last show—"great symbols of our emptiness."

Mari's self-portraits are of a woman in her studio. Sometimes the woman is reflected, always imperfectly, in a mirror; sometimes she is looking, from a mirror, at Greek sculpture; sometimes a body, an arm, is no more than hinted at and head and eyes are painted with intent detail, the paint built up to sculptural proportions in attempts to catch a fully plastic complexity; sometimes a face is blank or spare or merely an outline; sometimes the woman is multiplied by her own adumbration.

Looking at them in her show and then back in her vastly crowded studio, and thinking of them now, there on the crest of the bench, I think of other images of women in American art: the studied, posed, coolly indifferent and superior face of O'Keeffe in the Stieglitz photographs—a vision of Woman-on-Pedestal, Woman-as-Object-of-Beauty; de Kooning's richly grotesque monster women—and the fashion models and movie stars with whom they collide, whom they deride; Warhol's campy Marilyns, no Wonder Woman or idol to me, no object of fascination; Cindy Sherman's photographs of herself as Everyone Else—that careerist game heralded as the work of someone "who could be a great artist in any medium" . . . this pathetic bilge in high places, as if photographic stills could indicate much about skill in painting, sculpture, or macramé.

This woman in my wife's paintings, she who has been looking these past weeks at that landscape in front of us both, ain't none of the above. She is beyond irony, beyond poseur, beyond the mannered and the myth-made. She looks out from the canvases with questioning, doubt, determination, from her place of work, asking who she is and who you are, not intimidating or superior but herself. She is not a symbol or an emblem but the thing itself, a woman, a worker in the vineyards of art, earthy, half a dozen people, some opaque, some transparent, now a bit more defiant (and why not after so many years of intense work, slenderly seen by the world?), now firm, now a suppliant, now in the company of the old dead painters who live inside her—like Rembrandt's old self-portrait in the Louvre, which seems to say, "Here I am. I am no wiser. I am sadder, perhaps deeper. What I do is paint. Here is where I belong. In my earlier portraits I looked out at the world and said, 'I am myself, in fine garments. I can do anything.'" RvR appears in some of the paintings with her and also Cézanne, Beckmann, and Velázquez, whose *Juan de Pareja* she visits a dozen times a year. They're more her friends than the few people she knows. They listen and cheer her on. The paintings are either good paintings or not but these old guys are the best company. She is not playing games. She means it. She has reached the age of sixty and she doesn't know the name of a rock star or a talk-show host.

Her friend Carolee "invented an art" by pulling manifestos out of her crotch, to which Mari says: "To me, who worries about the history of art and anguishes over a red, a shape, such statements seem preposterous. Fuck it. So what? Pieces of paper with blood-red stains—whose blood? Does it really tell me anything about women or death, or anything?"

"Not any more than coins on the floor in the shape of a battle-ship tells me anything whatsoever about the relationship of money and war," I said, referring to Roberta Smith's pronounce-ment that this was profoundly so in Chris Burden's constructions. "Or a few twisted wires on a wall can be 'brilliant minimalist sculpture.'"

We were working our way into a big despair and enjoying the hostility toward gimmicks, tricks, wispy *fin de siècle* ironies, truism-cliché ironies on a neon strip, all the Sons and Daugh-ters of Dada, and were just ready to lambast the Cake Mas-ters School of pretty, delicious art, too, and Beaux Arts realism when I said, "Aw, let's go fishing. It's getting late. The caddis will—"

"Caddis!" she said. "You don't understand. You really don't. I may not buy what they're doing but I've tried. I look at all of it. All you want to do is go fishing."

I said quietly: "There's a lot more I like to do."

"Well, it doesn't seem so sometimes."

"Well, if you don't want to go fishing, why don't we see a movie in Bozeman," I said, and mentioned what was playing.

"Sounds heavy," she said. "When I go to a movie I like to see something like *Meet Me in St. Louis.* Life is too much like a Chekhov play."

And that seemed to end the conversation.

But what am I, an old professor, to make of it all? A prominent critic says in a prominent place that three words on a canvas, by a painter who ten years earlier taught a little high-school English, demonstrates a "lifelong love of language." Is this a joke? She says it with a straight face. No one smiles. It is an absurdity wrapped with the quiet imprimatur of *The New York Times.* But what can I think, who for twenty-five years taught the great book Melville scraped word by word from the interior of his brain, of these three monumental, emblematic words, this assertion that they demonstrate anything at all about language?

"There's almost nothing to the wall drawings of Sol LeWitt," a critic advises us, noting that they are "free of ego," really made by high-school students from "cryptic instructions"; and in the larger sense his "elimination of the art object was the starting point, not the end, of a visual language he continues to elaborate. Few postwar artists have so successfully mined the tension between seeing and nothingness."

Ah, nothingness.

That gargantuan stump in front of my window, now dusted and looking like a whale's hump again, looks real to me; and so do her paintings of it. Blank canvases, painted cigar boxes, smudges, doodles, scratches seem less than real. That fellow lays coins on the floor in the shape of a battleship and they really are not a profound statement about the interaction of capitalism and war. A few pedestrian words on a canvas really should not be taken as evidence of a lifelong love of language, dating from the years when the artist taught high-school English, and cannot by me, who taught that great wealth of verbal richness in Browne, Melville, Hopkins, Joyce. Benches in a circle are not "great primitive symbols," they're benches in a circle; a moving neon display that is able to "work" within the architectural limits of a great building is an absurdity.

Yes, Mari, I've looked, and when I see all the cartoons, the graffiti, the flatness, the petty ironies, the publicity-seeking bravura, it sure looks and smells like a clever con to me, cooked up in East Hampton, baked over cocktail and cocaine parties, supported by payoffs and tax scams and favors and vested interests, promoted by a klatch of artists who scratch one another's egoes.

I don't mind sounding like a crank. I have become a crank.

Actually, I'm quite happy to agree with the Children of Dada that the world is absurd, all will come to death, the coffee pot is not a coffee pot but a collection of atoms in motion. But I am less willing to say that a couple of painted cigar boxes on the floor are *about* "freedom from conventional iconography," are *about* "freedom from the tyranny of sculpted form."

Quelle tyranny. It makes me shiver to think of all the fascism in Henry Moore.

Mari may be, as she says, "as easy to promote as belladonna," but I'm still innocent enough to believe that painting is not "about" promoting at all. I once asked a friend of hers about a painter whose work seemed to me especially gimmicky but who had just won a major award. "You should see her work a room," I was told, and happened to go to the ceremony and saw her and she sure does, which is a kind of skill, even a wonder to watch.

It is hard, with such repeated evidence in prominent places, not to agree that great art is dead, originality is dead, and that both have been discredited. But with this old wife of mine, death and discrediting have taken a holiday—and so have tricks and mannerism and anecdotes, squiggles, flecks, scratches, upside-down figures, trompe l'oeil, slaps, scribbles, serendipitous splashes, nice big nothingness sandwiches. If you want cute ironies, glamour, trendiness, look everywhere else. Here is someone who does anguish about where to put an emerald green, a cerulean blue, who doesn't worry if "this is not an age of oil-on-canvas painting," who paints.

She has always painted. At age fifteen she heard that Max Beckmann was giving a summer course at Mills College, lied to her parents that she was taking a swimming program, and every night wet her bathing suit and wrapped it up in a damp towel. Beckmann looked and said, *"Gut, gut, mein Kind,"* and pointed and nodded, and Quappi translated a few words, and at the end of the summer she brought her parents to a room at the college filled with her first paintings.

A few years ago I visited the co-op gallery at which Mari shows, during one of her exhibitions of self-portraits. It was a hard time for us and I was especially anxious for the show to succeed. I liked sitting in the room.

Looking up from a novel I was reading, I saw a foot turn at the door and disappear. A few moments later, having hit the end of the hallway and bounced back, a short man in dark clothes hustled back down the hall, past the door, into the stairwell, and disappeared. Was it a critic I had chastised in a letter for some silly words he once wrote, and then met and, identifying myself, saw bolt from me as from a madman? How I wish I'd learn not to write such letters. I could not be sure. What an irony if it *was* him, if in visiting this show, sitting there, I had spooked an emissary of the Castle. It is hard enough to be a member of a co-op gallery, flush up against the world, vulnerable, without a buffering dealer, ignored by many of the magazines and newspapers and critics.

But there's one. He comes to the door, snaps a look of exactly four seconds, signs his name, and leaves. Ah, the brilliance! Four seconds by the clock and he has seen everything: structure, form, the texture of the paint, the architectonics, the fruit of all these years' work, all sixteen paintings, at forty-five feet, in four seconds. What vision. What economy. How I wish I had gifts like that. Or those of the critics who know *not* to come, that it surely cannot be worth their while.

A few people come—nine so far today, eighteen yesterday—and then the room is empty again, except for the sixteen paintings, which I have to myself and study with great care. I don't know how to play the stock market of current art tastes—but the work does not seem conceptual enough for one newspaper, nor postmodernist enough for another; it is not especially conservative; it is more "maximalist" than minimalist; it makes no political statements, pleads no causes but its own; it hasn't the "vital, new" appeal of the show of parking-meter forms down the hall, which has been packing 'em in. They are merely paintings, like bright hot flames in Plato's cave in the Caucasus, and that, for the moment, seems quite enough. The paintings on the wall seem to be what art is about—beyond the callow kid-stars, the "in" and the laid-back, the less-than-nothing blackness and the too-much-of-everything, the high-powered hucksters, the high-ticket sales—here in this room, with sixteen unsold paintings is what art means. Still, I wish I could have happier words for the artist when I call in my report. And shall I mention that fleeing figure, who might have been the critic I spooked, who might have been afraid to face this harmless old humanist lunatic alone in the room with sixteen paintings, who might have been the one who, finally, would let Mari into the sacred chambers but chose instead to turn on his heel, slip like some furtive thing down the stairwell, and vanish forever?

And now, even after a fire that destroyed all her early work, she has a thousand canvases and twice as many drawings and watercolors in that great room, two thousand miles from here, above H & H Bagels. When I ask her, here in Montana where one needs very little, what she needs most now, she says: "The usual salami: attention, money, fame, glory, a major gallery, an exhibition at the Modern. But I'll settle for some paper towels, big boy."

4 HER OTHER ENIGMA

> I hop about bewildered among my fellow men.
> They regard me with deep suspicion.
> —FRANZ KAFKA

It is a rainy day, and Mari is painting her Big Enigma, a brown hump like the mountain, me. She painted me before, nearly forty years ago, naked, at the college where we met. She was always partial to cheap models who did not have to be flattered—herself, me—and I was cheap as dirt, thin then, and would sit for a smile though I couldn't hold the pose for three minutes.

Now I am a mountain of a man, graying by the hour, but I can sit for days, a kind of *Sitzfleisch,* reading or fussing with a few sentences. Mari says under her breath that I have everything her regular models have, only more of it.

As I sit here in front of the window, still as Buddha or the Sphinx, where she can see the old mountain over my left shoulder, my head is suddenly a hive of disconnected thoughts, ranging back to that other time I posed for her, in the Zabriskie Mansion just inherited by Bard College. I had finished two years of Army service and had returned to school as a freshman; Keith Botsford, at the New School, had told me with some authority, "You're not dumb, Nick," and I had found that encouraging in the extreme and with his help had parlayed a batch of random readings into an acceptance—I had been asked if I'd read Hawthorne, Melville, Yeats, and a half dozen others, and had quietly answered "no" each time. "What *have* you read?" the admissions officer asked, and I told him quietly that I had read *Martin Eden,* a dozen Hemingway stories, a couple of Steinbeck novels, and all of Kafka. "Ah," he said, and admitted me and I began again, though I had a degree in economics from the University of Pennsylvania.

Moments from the forty years we've had of it together, the tension and the falling-offs, the quiet moments, nights of passion, delusions, illusions, and, with our four children and the great hungry city, the endless pressures of money, of a life crying, like the house of D. H. Lawrence's rocking-horse loser, "There must be more money."

I think of the phone call I got at Crown Publishers one afternoon, the sound of her voice, still clear, saying, "The apartment . . . fire . . . everyone all right. Come quickly, Nick. Come quickly." And the cab uptown to find the place we'd tried to build consumed in smoke, the sirens and lights, and ladders blasting my eye, our four children safe, the collie dead, and two days later the walk through that place: tilted black frames on the walls, their canvas scorched or gone; a library of books blackened, hosed; my typewriter a lump of molten metal; clothes black rags, toys charred, manuscripts destroyed, not a piece of furniture salvageable, the stink of wetness and smoke everywhere, the heat of the thing so severe that a chicken in the freezer had been roasted. I remember seeing the strong box, with the mark of a fireman's tool in its top, the papers inside burned and scattered, some jewelry and an heirloom watch swiped. My glass fly rods were burned, along with every fly I had in every plastic box; my reels were bent and blackened, vest burned through, though still on a nail, boots melted. But my mind comes back to the paintings; all but four or five she'd made from the age of fifteen until that time were destroyed—either in the racks we'd had built in the room she used for a studio, or those ghosts on the walls, askew, viscerated, like burned toast. We saved a few that the fire had only breathed on; one was out for framing; a couple were seared and we tried to save them but could not. And then she started again.

I remember taking all the children to school, able to hold the hands of only two, Charles racing across Seventy-ninth, between cars headed in opposite directions, my heart pounding out of my chest.

I remember the tug and strain of money. Two jobs were not enough. Nor three. Checks bounced. I borrowed to the last nickel of my credit. I borrowed from Crown, my employer, and from Hunter College, shackling myself to them. I did ghostwriting. For nights on end. One child remembered me working all night dozens of times; it was more. I sold books and rods—and I tried to keep writing, to let Mari paint, to keep children from slipping off the edge of the universe into pool hall or mediocrity.

And then, suddenly, all the decades gone and we are here on the bench and I am still in love and still love to fuss around rivers and have written twenty-odd books, if you include some without my name on them, and I come, as I always come, to the heavy brand of self-examination I always descend to. Just this morning, like Joyce's Gabriel, I passed a mirror and wanted to distance myself from the fatuous fool who bearded me—with his pretensions and clownishness, his self-deprecating words, his innocent fear of politics and computers, his sentimentalizing of sport. He was a dowdy fellow, as far from fashion and glamour as one might get, and he thought immediately of Marlene Dietrich's pronouncement: "Glamour is assurance." (Just what I'm full of.) "It is a kind of knowing that you are all right in every way, mentally and physically" (how then?) "and in appearance" (me?) "and that whatever the occasion or the situation, you are equal to it." The comment astounds me. Glamour? It is what changes in an hour, like taste, like the aura of the Sphinx, not the Sphinx itself. Glamour? I'm lucky to be here, to finish each day, and though I might admire the lilting elegance of Astaire, that throaty confidence of Dietrich, who mostly thought herself "all right in every way" and in the end wouldn't have others know otherwise, what I know, in my bones, is the stutter of my heart, the grunting struggle to know what has happened, what is happening to me, the rage to feel, to say, against the tug of a recalcitrant tongue, a perplexed brain. Many years ago, art said to me, like Rilke's archaic torso of Apollo, "You must change your life." I tried. I beat the hesitant words into stories and poems and in despair threw them out. I found little capacity to invent. The world in which I lived was too strange, palpable, evanescent, terrifying to need the other. For mortal enemy I always had the IRS; for fear, a child running between two cars or, due home, heading for the Middle East; and for anxiety, money, always money—enough to pay the rent, cover the check I wrote last week, yesterday, meet tuition. I felt like my neighbors were Bouchers, Fragonards, and I was Chardin's *The Ray*—that visceral, haunting, smiling fish, hung on a hook, sliced open, the cat ready to pounce, varied sea creatures opened too, the knife nearby.

I began to think more and more about the art I could admire. It was not that of Rodin, whom I had loved in my early twenties. He was a great man, all right, a cock-of-the-walk, and took the world with a postured hedonism, lived high on the hog, won most of the awards his time could offer. His mistress, Camille Claudel, who went mad, interested me more; Degas's unheroic horses and dancers touched me more deeply; van Gogh, who killed himself from despair, sold nothing, is vastly his superior.

Why, I wondered, was I more attracted to the anguished, urgent cry of the coyote caught in a trap, the artist pleading always and desperately and only for survival. It was such an unpleasant sound. Perhaps the *dulce* part of art has been overrated, along with the *utile*.

And for all that, despite my abiding love for Kafka, who was surely right in knowing that the numbers never add correctly, my own writing has always leaned toward the light anecdote, the feel of the creek, the dance of words, not aspiring to even the seriousness of Hemingway's "Big Two-Hearted River" but more for the fun he actually had on the Fox River in September 1919 with a couple of pals.

I am in my mid-sixties and I still take my emotional temperature a couple of times each hour. And I must be a hedonist of the first water for loving this pursuit of brown trout on spring creeks so much.

So, sitting near the window, looking at Sphinx Mountain and at my frizzy-haired wife, thinking of days past, landscapes, brush and canvas, East and West, this and that, my unaccountable love of fishing, I suddenly start scribbling away on some yellow notepads I always keep handy.

Mari does not look away from the canvas or from me but asks, with some irritation, what I am scribbling so ferociously. Must I do everything with such intensity? I tell her it's a chapter in a little book about my odd secret life with fishing books. The chapter is called "Bergman in Brooklyn."

"Ingmar?" she asks, without looking up.

"Ray!"

"You sure are scribbling hard. Noisy, too."

"I am the Balzac of the bench!" I proclaim.

"Sure," she says, making certain that she flatters me neither in word nor image. "You make Balzac look like Abraham Lincoln."

5 IN THE STONE HOUSE

> Indeed, we are but shadows: we are not endowed with
> real life, all that seems most real about us is but the
> thinnest substance of a dream—till the heart be
> touched. That touch creates us—then we begin to be.
> —NATHANIEL HAWTHORNE,
> in a letter to Sophia

It is a freakish house—a squarish old stone structure, built many years ago to generate power from nearby Blaine Spring Creek, to sell to the few other houses on the bench. The powerhouse is only a short walk from the Downing House and it does not have the same view, though the Sphinx is visible from one of the long thin windows in the living room, and from any of several slight rises in the land in front of the house. A local kitchen-and-bathroom-fixture salesman bought it more than a dozen years ago and appears to have used whatever spare fixtures were available, what he could get at a bargain price—or else he had a weird sense of design. Except for a huge, well-turned, modern kitchen, the fixtures are quirky in the extreme, a garish mixture of kitschy brass, rooms from the cheapest motels in town, colors found chiefly in cathouses.

None of that matters. The main room is thirty or more feet high, and we like space. Blaine Spring Creek—tumbling too fast to fish—is out back and there are three ponds cantilevered behind the house, the highest taking water from the creek and passing it to the middle pond, and the lowest returning it to Blaine. From the bedroom over the kitchen extension, we can hear the rushing creek all night, and if we lean out those windows we can see the ponds, often with trout rising.

I have my seven fly rods, vests, boots, and jackets on nails in the garage, near the woodpile, on which I've placed twenty-odd fly boxes and other paraphernalia; Mari keeps all of her art supplies out there, too, on the large wooden tool table. She paints only outside, except now and then when it's windy and she works in the open garage. We were here last autumn for a few weeks and she painted the umber hayfields on the Varney Road and the autumn colors behind Doc Losee's house—alizarin, crimson, aurelian, the tawny reds of horse chestnuts, which reminded me of upstate New York and the first season I fell in love. The fishing was poor. I floated the Madison with Vaughan several times and came up nearly empty. I know now that something called whirling disease has killed a large proportion of the rainbow trout, though the browns—always my favorites—are apparently immune.

We've been fishing here a week and I've been working steadily at a table I set up near the front door. With masking tape, Mari has put three watercolors on the stone walls of the

main room and has just started her first oil. The work is different, and I am watching it carefully. Now and again a doe and her two spotted fawns slip tentatively across the field in front of me, headed for high green grasses near the pond. Twice I heard a clicking sound, like pebbles thrown hard against tin, and found outside a trembling flicker, its neck broken from having flown full force into a window. I gave one bird to a friend, to make flies from; another I left where it fell and within an hour some creature had recycled the feckless bird.

The deaths of the flickers trouble me not at all. I've seen enough death over the past years and it has rather gotten into my blood that death comes for the archbishop and Ivan Ilyich and every little and large thing in its own time. My sister—ten years my junior—died while I was speaking to her on the telephone one morning thirteen years ago; I heard the death gurgle, rushed to her apartment, and found her lying on the floor, still clutching the phone, her Yorkie barking behind a barrier. Like Everyman, I don't care to be forward about it myself, and several years ago almost slipped away. I had been feeling weak for a month and had attributed it merely to a bit too much work, a bit of age, the onset of still more weight after a severe weight loss. Then one day at lunch with a pleasant fellow I'd wanted for a year to meet, I raised a fork and barely had the strength to hold it up. A day later, after my doctor diagnosed the problem as the flu, I passed out and was hauled to the hospital feet first with a failing pulse, jaundice, a clogged bile duct—all from a gall bladder that had gone berserk. After eleven days on intravenous antibiotics my various organs calmed down enough so they could pluck out my gall bladder, which they said was "fried to my liver."

And then Mari developed alarming symptoms: periodic bouts of severe abdominal pain, total nausea, and radical weight loss. She took batteries of tests, then more batteries of unpleasant tests, then got widely varying diagnoses, and switched doctors a few times; one doctor called me paranoid for wanting to see the CAT scans; another shouted at Mari; all, after a lifetime of good health, seemed like mere money-grubbing technicians to me. Just before we came out she finally had abdominal surgery. But the pains and weight loss continued, the CAT scans found more tumors, and then old Doc Losee from down the road came over one evening a week ago. He touched and listened with naked ear; he dropped to the floor beside her bed and listened more, his ear to her spleen. A half hour later he spotted a neck goiter that all the New York specialists had missed. It surely means hyperthyroid disease, which probably accounts for her severe weight loss. That, at least, is treatable, and the tumors have all proved benign. Every surgeon in New York has wanted to operate and we—and Losee—resist such quick-draw artists. Mari says: "They look at my ovaries and see their next trip to Caracas." Losee stayed two hours, the last hour to be sure *I* was all right, and then I walked him outside at 1:30 and he paused to show me the Milky Way and half a dozen constellations. Just like the New York doctors would have done.

So we're feeling a touch of mortality this summer and with the river damaged by its disease, we're sticking close to this big old house. We still watch the Sphinx and Mari has painted it, but she is becoming more and more interested in the ponds, with their overhanging branches, deadfalls and dying trees, reflections, and patches of light. She had been working steadily behind the powerhouse, facing the creek, and on the rim of the ponds. Here in the West, without boundaries, she was at first attracted to the vastness of the place, buffered by a dozen different skies each hour, the light, the sense that we are both smaller and larger here, that all is in flux—even the mountain, surely the cloud formations and colors in the sixty-mile sky, and the colors the sky imputes to slope and field, water and mountain peak. Now the ponds, which are more intimate, contained, even magical, seem to combine all she has sought here.

The new work seems closer to John Marin's landscapes than anything I've seen of hers in recent years, breaking up the forms to register the effects of a flickering world, imposing maverick color, finding a happy animation in the scene. We both think Marin may be the finest, surely the freest, of the American landscape painters, with his nonrhetoric, vital, and earthy paintings. He has the verse and innocent delight of Gershwin, the originality of something free-form and vigorous. He is far from the lovely grays, the gentle light of Corot's happy pieties, and farther still from the darknesses of Ryder, the exotic flatness of Gaugin. And so is Mari. We both love the intimate, loving details of Constable's charming renderings of the charming Stour Valley, and I have fished there and it is in itself, with its quiet meadows and old stone and wooden mills, that charming still— though Mari would not paint it that way; we are not charming and her work is not charming. I have got to brooding about what she's doing and what it means.

Nature is neither a terrifying, awesome spectacle to her nor a studied garden, an emblem of what men can carve out of the chaotic universe, what money built at Giverny. She sees no hieroglyphs in the mountains, like Sir Thomas Browne's quincunx, in his Garden of Cyrus, to be mystically considered, nor any necessary fantasy. What harmonies there are come from her choice of sections of a landscape, or, more specifically, from harmony, dissonance possible in the canvas itself. In some ways, I suppose, this selection reflects her temperament, but she so painstakingly eschews mannerism of all kinds that I am hard put to leave looking at one of her new pond paintings or Sphinx Mountain paintings and say these are *about* some aspect of her temperament. I suspect the gnarled agitation in van Gogh and repetitions of form in Cézanne are mostly what they are but are also generous to the critics looking for lunacy in a swirl and mother's teat on a mountaintop. Critics, like reporters, need something new to say, need news; often there is not enough that is news (as Pound has it) and stays news, so they make profound statements out of twisted wires, nickels, cigar boxes. Psychology, defined and defining symbolism seem inappropriate when I look at Mari's new work; yet every stroke of them is in some way "symbolic."

There is in El Greco's *View of Toledo* and Giorgione's *La Tempesta* landscape imbued with Christian foreboding. I do not think she has imputed to sky or field the harsh correlatives of feeling, the swirls of *The Starry Night* or the richly orchestrated feast of a Turner sunset or fire. She does not want to impose her feelings upon the landscape or to use the landscape for special effects, or political statements; nor will she be decorative or ingratiating. Ah, dear. "Artists build theories round what they would like to do," says Malraux, "but they do what they can."

Cézanne more than any other painter has been her teacher. I have seen her stand before *Le Chateau Noir,* the paintings of L'Estaque—so blue and evanescent—Mont Sainte-Victoire, the interior landscapes of rocks and pines for hours. We have seen his mountain and his *Jas de Bouffan,* and we once spent a silent afternoon in his studio outside of Aix, taking in everything from the still-life props to the slit in the wall through which his large bathers must have exited. At times I have seen traces of his faceting, his simplification of forms in Mari's work—but I think she has been less interested in isolated aspects of technique than in a total relationship to the landscape from him: something quietly reverential of that thing outside of her, something that would become the amanuensis, the instrument of making art. She admires the good Pissarro but I see little of him in what she does; Renoir and Courbet and the illustrative Homer and fifty others are in her head, always of some degree of interest, but they do not teach. The Sphinx teaches. Marin teaches. Cézanne is always with her. The canvas teaches.

Painters are not allotted one style, like a dance card, to fill up; nor is the antidote, "style," something that should then inform all else. Everything she does it tempered by the cold fact that she comes after the bright improvisations of Kandinsky, the kaleidoscopic invention of Marin, the dissolution of Cézanne in cubism and abstract expressionism. She is not moving toward abstraction, like the nineteenth- and early-twentieth-century painters—toward that moment when water-lilies become circles become blur—but mediating the claims of that exhilarating life of pure form and the specific pond beyond the specific stone house. Once an abstract painter, she has come back, tenuously, with a constant tension between both worlds, to the image, using the field of hay, the depth of umber in an autumn field, the lifelikeness, airiness of treetops touched by breeze, as a place to begin, a place not finally to leave. There is a rich indefiniteness in abstraction, an intimate specificity and psychological intensity in figuration. In the end, the world is too palpable, too various in its forms, too improbable to be denied, and the life of abstract forms is too various, too full of possibility, to be denied.

And so as I sit here she walks onto the mound beside the pond, sets up her easel, fixes the canvas, squeezes out her paints upon a long sheet of wax paper, and starts still again from white. Her movements are at first tentative, as if she is still not fully incarnate, as if she's a guest in her body. Her loss of thirty pounds has made her wraithlike. But as she adjusts the easel slightly, then adjusts it again, then fixes a section of this new vista in her eye, she becomes more deliberate, marking the pond and the bent tree in her mind, then fixing those two forms onto the canvas with several bold strokes of her brush, touched with Mars brown. Warm colors next to cool next to warm. Push and pull. The reflections endemic to water, not to earth. Always, as in de Kooning, the whole. Now she is more fully herself, now she enters that dance, that triangle between her, the world, and the canvas and becomes fully alive in her intensity, even as she struggles not to *express* something but to make the recalcitrant canvas take wing, breathe, and sing.

* * *

My friend Ted Leeson has taken the octagonal house down the Gravelly Range Road. He has been fishing hard and I have been listening patiently to his reports—most of them glum—even as I beg off my old madness for fishing, claim to be puritanical in the extreme about getting a few words on paper, and probably am. It has been a long year and I am straining at the leash of my book-publishing "trade," which Thoreau says must lead down. I am trying not to cleanse myself of it but to start other engines that, per force, I have turned to quarter speed or idle. This writing is dangerous. It "nibbles at the soul"; it is jealous in the extreme.

But Ted says that the river has been dropping, so I agree to go off with him and his brother and we gather up his drift boat and our equipment, and float the Madison, trying to find some evidence that the biologists are wrong, that the whirling disease is exaggerated, as those with vested interests in tourists say. It is not. After several hours of it, fishing on the top and fishing deep, using caddis pupae and Humpies and even flies attached by leader tied to the shank of the top fly, I have caught nothing. Then from a riffle at the corner of an island, I get a heavy strike on the dropper fly and feel the weight of the first good fish of the season. It is a brown, about seventeen inches' worth, and it has taken the fly Ted said it would, which I'd claimed could not draw a strike.

It is the brown trout, the foreigner to this country, the greater foreigner to the American West, where it was ridiculed and called German brown and loch leven, that saves us now and that proves the greatest of the trouts: cautious, doubting, self-protecting, to be caught only by the proper fly at the proper time, unpredictable in its fight, resistant to disease. The native cutthroat has been vastly diminished by profligate generosity, and the transplanted brookie—gorgeous to the extreme—is too generous as well. The grayling is almost gone and the rainbow, from farther west, was resisted here and then accepted with full heart for its bright silver and its leaps, but is slaughtered by the mysterious parasite now. The brown survives. The brown is the new native, beyond the failing concept of native. The brown pleases me just fine.

With a week of dry, warm weather, the grasshoppers have been coming down from the highest, driest benches to the green bottomland near Spring Creek. I fished with Sandy a few days ago and had a marvelous time of it, splatting a good hopper imitation up against a far bank, into the current seams, against the points of the "S" curves; and the fish came readily to our flies—big, wild browns, spotted like the ocelot, unselective, greedy now, and very strong. There was an ampleness, a bold simplicity to the day, a fullness that heralded the unthinkable, sensuous fun that fly fishing now and then provides.

A few fish go a long way with me lately. The day filled me and let me turn back to some writing and some quiet prowling near the old stone house, especially up to the ponds.

All of the connected ponds contain wild browns that have come in from Blaine Spring Creek: the large open pond at the top, which holds the most; the middle pond, in which trout rise in small patches of clear water, between masses of weeds,

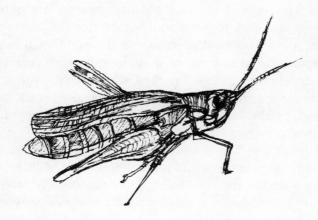

and could be hooked but not brought to hand; and the lower pond, the dark one, thalo blue and deep and intense, under the cottonwoods, not thirty feet from our garage—which interests both Mari and me most. We can fish it together, mingling fishing and art, which Marin found "one and the same thing" with him. Mari, of course, doesn't. She laughs at the notion.

At a spot near the east side of the pond, Mari sets up her easel where she can see the entire pond, the angled colossus of a cottonwood (dead except for a half dozen improbable branches of green), the high grasses to the south, and then the ochre mountains and pale-blue sky to the west, through the trees. She loves to paint there and frequently comes down to the house and announces that she's seen a merganser, some deer over for a drink at midday, the circles of trout rising. Wasn't I interested in the rising trout? Was something wrong?

I had seen the circles. They were not the sort of phenomenon my eyes missed. I had seen them the first day of our visit and, walking completely around the pond, I also saw a dozen darting shapes—long, skittery wraiths—some less than ten inches, a few closer to twenty. I found it very satisfying to have any kind of water so close at hand—especially water that held wild brown trout.

Soon I was walking up the short embankment three or four times a day, to peek through the high grasses out onto the surface of the dark lower pond. Sometimes the surface was broken by wind, even whitecaps, but it could be flat as glass, too, especially in the early morning or at dusk. Several times, naked except for slippers, I walked out before the sun was up and was always greeted, ten steps before I could see it fishing my pond, by the flight of the most lethal trout-fisher of all, a huge great blue heron.

The pond was handy and I did not at first think seriously about fishing it. It was a complete, self-contained little world of its own, and at first I just wanted to understand its laws a bit better, even as Mari was finding in it a mysterious world of

forms, shadows, and reflections, an animated totality in sharp contrast to the solidity of the Sphinx. For the Sphinx, despite all those changes it seemed to undergo, was surely as solid and monumental as a Mont Sainte-Victoire or a Kilimanjaro, and not emblematic of change but of permanence, as Mont Saint-Victoire must have been for Cézanne, who painted it sixty times and created it—each time different but each drawing on the permanence, serenity, not any evanescence in the structure. Even the nature of her paintings is different: those of the mountain dominated by that imposing structure, those of the pond seeking movement.

Yes, Mari is surely interested in movement—the intimate play of light and shadow, the vital aliveness of the entire canvas, like a Pollock or Guston, fully orchestrated. Her sketches have an overall intensity and joy to them; without anything studied or hesitant in them, they capture the multiple perspectives that are natural for an active eye. There are quick strokes and dramatic juxtapositions of blue and white and yellow; her eyes seem to see the whole scene at once and, simultaneously, its isolated moments.

For me, I simply wanted to know a bit more about the fish and aquatic insects that live in the pond, when they share their mystery with me; and I wanted to understand the creatures that live on its periphery and use the pond for their special purposes, even as I thought of what harmless uses I might make.

I had fished the Madison with Ted, Spring Creek with grasshoppers with Sandy, full of the larger quarry for which I'd come to this part of the world. Sometimes they were generous, sometimes not—which is as it should be. They always demanded some special expenditure of energy to drive to, float down, walk to, pursue. I had days when I saw only small fish—or nothing; several that offered too many big fish; and then, after my great grasshopper day I turned my attention fully to the pond.

We shared it.

Mari painted there at midday, I fished it at the extremities of the day. It was smaller—no more than a quarter acre—but it reminded me of Ice Pond, the sump where I caught bluegill and perch when I was six and seven, at a boarding school, and for some reason I suddenly decided to fish it in the old way, with a bobber and live bait. Mari feigned shock when I bought a dozen nightcrawlers at the market and put them into our refrigerator, as I once did after I'd plucked them from lawns in Peekskill and, later, Brooklyn. I blithely ignored her when she proclaimed that I was a great embarrassment to her, that she'd tell all of my fly-fishing friends.

I bought a spinning rod and reel, the first I'd owned in thirty years, a red-and-white plastic bobber, and a couple of No. 16 hooks.

She shook her head sadly when I carried one of the white lawn chairs up from the house to the rim of the lower pond

and set it squarely behind some high grasses. "Fly fishing," I muttered to her as I passed, "is degenerating into an art form. I'm returning to my roots."

"You're using W-O-R-M-S," she shouted, "and I'm going to tell *everyone*."

I set the chair deep in the grasses, so I'd be out of sight, baited the hook with a large nightcrawler, and lobbed a cast out into the pool. The bobber and worm made a tremendous ker-plunk when they hit, I waited patiently for twenty minutes, then reeled in, checked my untouched bait, and cast again. You would have thought there wasn't a fish within miles. I didn't have a touch or a bump. The little red-and-white globe perched motionless on the surface of the small pond, moving only when a breeze ruffled the surface. Mari came from her easel, set up near the creek twenty-five feet away, and asked: "Cleaned 'em out yet, big boy?"

For the first ten minutes, full of expectation, I had been quite pleased with myself, very much at ease. Then I grew a bit restless and began to think about whether my line was too heavy, the worm too big, the bait deep enough. I might have made changes. I might have pursued the couple of dozen trout I knew were in the pond with more tenacity. But the truth is, I soon grew bored silly by my return to innocence, and in less than an hour I left my blind, took the white chair back to the garage,

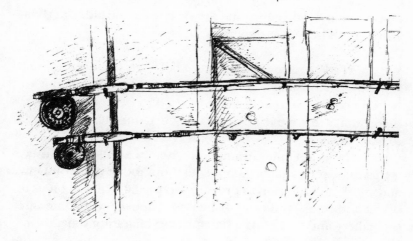

and went at once to all my fly rods, horizontal on nails hammered into the wall of the garage. I had half a dozen rods. I took down the lightest of them, a No. 4, tied on a 7X leader and a Mathews X-Caddis, had myself a long beer, and slipped heronlike to the pond again, a half hour later.

Shadows now covered most of the surface, which, with the reflections, was alive in a hundred ways. Mari had made a dozen watercolors and oils of the pond; I felt I might have been in one of her paintings. One of the ways in which the pond was alive, which she would have missed, was the number of dancing caddis above the water, like I'd seen half a dozen times before. I watched for a few moments in the muggy evening, saw two of the biggest fish in the pond—fish I knew were better than seventeen inches—come crashing out, pulverizing the surface. When the water settled down I made a long false cast over land, pivoted, and pitched the fly where the last trout had risen. The X-Caddis came down gently to the surface of the pond and a trout took it at once. Then, using all the sophisticated skills I could muster, I caught three trout in the next twenty minutes, and turned them back, until the bats began to dive-bomb me. The heron and the seven-year-old kid I once was would have been less generous.

We are ready to leave this place where we came to transact some private business. We were not here for very long but we were here together, and we have tried to be good friends to this country that we have come to love, to take it inside us and to leave it alone.

Two thousand miles from here, where we will return, there is that huge room full of canvases, a thousand or more of them, and another exhibition to prepare for; the fall will call on us to select and frame and then display to whoever will come into the gallery and look. It is a harsh but exhilarating time.

It is only four years since the first of the watercolors meta-morphosed into the mammoth landscapes there, painted two thousand miles from Montana, mostly from memory, some as large as seven feet by eight feet, the diptychs larger, made from an inner eye, and the watercolors at Eightieth Street and Broad-way, over a bagel-baking shop. Now there are fifty of them, some made in Ennis, some where you cannot see the Sphinx, some where it blasts your eye, some where it is a lump on a faraway silhouette. This fall I expect she will take these new "Ponds" and "Treetops" in watercolor and small oil-on-canvas paintings and make large oils, too—with that new overall ani-mation and vigor, that fascination with what is totally alive, in motion, rather than that which, even with its temporal changes, is an inevitable emblem for the haunting solidity we all want, artists most. She seems to have cut all moorings; after all that she's made, these ponds and treetops are fresh and new. She is younger than ever.

There is a world somewhere and it does not much think of her. "I have lower abdominal pains, nausea, and lumps on my toes," she told me this morning. "And I'm invisible." But *I* think of her and try to see her, and she thinks of me and about that mountain and the ponds, and the mountain and ponds on her canvases and paper. Nearly forty years ago, in a dark car, I told her, unable to look to my right for her reaction, all the words that fleshed out cryptic letters in a diary I later destroyed— emblems of events I could not write out, my nether soul, be-cause I did not think I could have a life with her or anyone if I were not known, like the bearish Levin in *Anna Karenina*, in my deepest core, I who was no one yet. How I wished, with Quintilian, that the heart truly made the eloquence; but my words were only coarse and dumb, shattering the wooing tones of the prior three months. We made choices that night. We set a course. She made the most dramatic choice of her life when she turned to me. All the fights, the falling-offs, the fear, the love, the imperfect fit of people different but often enough one, the movement closer and closer, to where I am, where she is, were ordained that night. When I was done and she turned to me and put out her hand and touched me, that touch made me live.

And now, well down the road, she says, "Well, if you have raised four children and stayed married to a *fish-er-man* for nearly forty years, I guess you can do anything."

Before I pack for the trip, I take a hard look at the canvases she has made this summer—eighteen of them, and five portfolios of watercolors—ready to be crated and shipped UPS from the True Value store in Ennis. To my left, below the Gravellies, is the pond that Mari has been painting; it is contained, more intimate than most of Montana, but it has its lien on wildness, too. And the paintings of the pond are full of light and shadow, reflection and evanescence. I have not learned everything but I have learned some things about her paintings.

Across the valley, then the river, then another bench, and on above the foothills, there is Sphinx Mountain. It's still there. It looks solid as rock. But it's having one of its red days.

TAILPIECE:
A FLY FISHER'S GIFTS

Another holiday season is approaching, the end of another year, and I have been thinking of what gifts to give to a dozen fly-fishing friends, and that has led me to think of a whole ark of gifts I've received over a score of years, and about gift-giving generally.

"Give what you'd like to receive," goes one maxim—and it's a good one, unless you like girdle bugs and your friend fishes only No. 22 Blue-Winged Olives, or vice versa. "Give what you think your friend will like" is another—though this often takes a fair bit of hard thought, and some searching, and a bit more knowledge of friends than people of a "Me! Now!" generation generally possess; and the wrong gift may very well lead to questions about whether you know your old friend at all after all these years, and why not.

If you give too stingy a gift, it may draw ire—"Is that *all* I mean to him—two lousy Woolly Buggers?" Too expensive a gift—a Bogdan reel, perhaps—may breed suspicion that you're trying to buy something, perhaps a nine-week visit to his ranch, where the trout are half again as long as your leg.

You can insult or enrage through carelessness, and baffle or startle or surprise or please. The more I think about it, the harder this simple act becomes, the more fraught with potholes, some potentially lethal to a friendship.

Yet I have taken immense pleasure from hundreds of gifts, small and large, and am the least picky of receivers. I am the most graceful of takers.

I once fished a great deal with the late Mike Migel and he never once failed to give me the better pool or run to fish, the more productive riffle. Another, thought gruff or cold by a few folk I've met who barely knew him, did likewise, many times— usually by fussing with his line to show me conclusively that he could not possibly fish at this time to that steady riser at the upper end of the feeding lane, even if he wanted to do so. I was never fooled by either of them . . . and I took their gifts without guilt.

Lew Terwilliger, a master fly tier, has sent me three or four boxes crammed with his marvelous soft-hackle flies, and they give me great delight to look at and always take fish.

Craig Mathews always includes a few of his new patterns with his letters, and they keep me a few steps ahead of the rest of the world and in clover. I am mad for flies and can never get enough of them. I don't have enough of Tap Tapply's hair bugs to fish one, though that is that good and practical man's desire, but I sure enjoy looking at them on a cold November evening and they help me think of some fetching bass water I know.

My friend Justin once had a metalworker design a device that would without fail allow me to put small leader tippets through minuscule fly eyes. The only problems were that the hole in the device was not much larger than the eye of the fly and that the device itself was so small that I kept dropping it in the grass and then having to spend a half hour to find it, which I finally didn't. A third hand would have been useful—one for the tippet, one for the fly, one for the time- and labor-saving and eye-saving device. But the *thought* sure meant a lot to me.

I had to sell my library about fifteen years ago and now and then some good soul will just send one of those books back to me—just like that; a few of the other books I've retrieved at auctions—gifts to myself. Those people didn't have to do that—and the knowledge that they didn't somehow makes the gifts sweeter.

There's a lot of feeling and sentiment tied up in a gift—when it's given, by whom, and sometimes why and even how.

When my apartment was burned flat down to charcoal—including waders, flies, reels, rods, and just about everything else—the late Frank Mele gave me an old Payne rod, one of his favorites, to start me fishing again. After I'd sold all of my bamboo rods and thought I'd given up that lovely wood forever, George Maurer gave me one that he'd made—a seven-foot, nine-inch beauty for a No. 5 line, quick and strong and delicate, as the best dry-fly rods should be; and he gave me not only that rod but a renewed love of fine bamboo, for he's a superb rodmaker.

Ted Leeson, and Dave Whitlock, and Len Wright, and Matt Supinski, and Carl Richards, and Doug Swisher, and Alec Jackson, knowing my insatiable addiction to those feathered things, my curiosity about their architectonics, have all given me flies that I'll take out half a dozen times a year and spread on my long oak dining table, fingering every one of them with glee, for I am a fly miser of the first water. And I do likewise with flies given me by Dick Talleur, Tatsuhiro Saido, Art Scheck, Lou Tabory, Tom Rosenbauer, Lefty Kreh, Neil Patterson, John Goddard, Skip Morris, Darrel Martin, Bob Boyle, Larry Duckwall, Will Ryan, Steve Meyers, Chuck Reed, and dozens of others.

It may seem happier to take all this stuff than to give, but I am a compulsive giver. Three days after I buy a dozen pert Sparkle-Dun Sulphurs from Ken Meade I give away six, because (a) twelve seems potentially greedy and surely more than I need this spring, and (b) Sandy and Bob can definitely use a few good Sulphurs this season. In fact, I can barely imagine them surviving May without a few of my deadly Sulphurs.

Water feels like a gift to me. And so do the trout and bass and fluke that inhabit it. And so do the mayflies, and skunk cabbage, and trillium, and willows, and lilies, and lily pads, and so do old fly-fishing books, gifts from an earlier day, from author-fishermen who gave what they wrote.

More than rods and flies, more than a given tortuga of a trout, I love that gift of words. I have been writing about fishing—

with one brief interlude—for thirty years or thereabouts. Doing so has multiplied the pleasure I take from fishing, especially fly fishing, a thousandfold, allowing me to relive golden days and hours of buffoonery, little triumphs and wild imaginings. How could my old friend Clyde ever have been born had I not taken some of the more bizarre traits of several friends, and of myself, and whipped him up from that stew?

I'm grateful to the scores of readers who have written to me, to tell me that this or that bit of my writing touched them, or made them laugh, or who shared their point of view. I treasure such gifts, especially since I have been at such pains to make my words dance.

Another season of gifts is upon me now and I merely want to say, from my heart, thanks to all you fly fishers who have given me, time and again over these many years, the gift of your eyes . . . and heart.